Darkness Is Golden

A Guide To Personal Transformation And Dealing With Life's Messiness

Mary Hoang

16pt

Read How You Want
LARGE PRINT BOOKS, BRAILLE & DAISY

PANTERA PRESS

The information in this book is published in good faith and for general information purposes only. Although the author and publisher believe at the time of going to press that the information is correct, they do not assume and hereby disclaim any liability to any party for any loss, damage or disruption caused by errors or omissions, whether they result from negligence, accident or any other cause.

First published in 2021 by Pantera Press Pty Limited
www.PanteraPress.com

Text Copyright © Mary Hoang, 2021
Mary Hoang has asserted her moral rights to be identified as the author of this work.
Design and Typography Copyright © Pantera Press Pty Limited, 2021

® Pantera Press, three-slashes colophon device, and *sparking imagination, conversation & change* are registered trademarks of Pantera Press Pty Limited. Lost the Plot is a trademark of Pantera Press Pty Limited.

This work is copyright, and all rights are reserved. Apart from any use permitted under *Copyright legislation*, no part may be reproduced or transmitted in any form or by any means, nor may any other exclusive right be exercised, without the publisher's prior permission in writing. We welcome your support of the author's rights, so please only buy authorised editions.

Please send all permission queries to:
Pantera Press, P.O. Box 1989, Neutral Bay, NSW 2089, Australia or info@PanteraPress.com
A Cataloguing-in-Publication entry for this book is available from the National Library of Australia.

Cover design: Luke Bird
Author photo: Max Doyle
Publisher: Lex Hirst
Editor: Elena Gomez
Proofreaders: Kirsty van der Veer and Anne Reilly
Typesetting: Kirby Jones
Original music and audio experiences: Rich Lucano (Phondupe)
Printed and bound in Australia by McPherson's Printing Group

TABLE OF CONTENTS

INTRODUCTION: Step into the Dark	v
CHAPTER 1: The Light in the Haunted House	1
CHAPTER 2: Monsters and Skeletons	36
CHAPTER 3: 'I Just Want to Be Happy'	69
CHAPTER 4: The Path Through Inner Conflict	112
CHAPTER 5: What Do You Need?	148
CHAPTER 6: How About 'No'?	194
CHAPTER 7: Breaking Your Patterns and Dropping the Baggage	224
CHAPTER 8: Mining the Darkness for Gold	261
CHAPTER 9: A Thousand Deaths	300
CONCLUSION: Homeward Bound	329
WORKS CITED	337

For my dad

QR CODE

To access the audio experiences, scan the QR code with your smart phone.

Alternatively, visit www.darknessisgolden.com/audio and follow the prompts.

AUDIO EXPERIENCES

Music is a central component of *Darkness is Golden.* Throughout this book, you will be engaging in the audio experiences contained in two playlists:

Playlist 1: Darkness is Golden: Audio Experiences Original meditations and sonic embodiments *Playlist 2: Darkness is Golden: Music for Reading* Curated music to accompany your reading experience

Instructions:

1. To access all of the above audio, open the scanner app on your smart phone camera, hold it over the QR code and follow the prompts. Alternatively, visit: www.darknessisgolden.com/audio

2. For ease of access, save the two playlists (*Darkness is Golden: Audio Experiences* and *Darkness is Golden: Music for Reading*) in Spotify. If this is not possible, bookmark the page www.darknessisgolden.com/audio in your browser.

3. Whenever you see the headphone symbol 🎧, go to your saved playlist *Darkness is Golden: Audio Experiences* and find the corresponding track number or visit www.darknessisgolden.com/audio

4. For an optimal experience, please use headphones when listening. *Darkness is Golden: Music for Reading* is a curated playlist designed to accompany your journey through the book. Hit play on this playlist now and whenever you continue reading.

INTRODUCTION

Step into the Dark

There are two sides to the messiness of life: life itself is messy, but so are we humans. At times, life is a complete shit show. No matter how much we try to control our lives, no matter how much we plan and safeguard, or seek stability, unpredictable and difficult things happen. We're also experts at ruining a good thing by overthinking – we love to complicate situations by (incorrectly) judging or overanalysing them. It's a conundrum: life throws us spanners, but we can often be the spanner ourselves.

Dealing with the messiness of life can be painful. Experiencing disappointment, heartbreak and failure hurts. Confronting your judgmental mind and vulnerabilities can make you feel sad and afraid, which is why we avoid doing so.

This avoidance of pain is a very human tendency: evolution has conditioned us to steer clear of pain where possible. Pain is a signal for danger and possible death; it is what helps us pull back from the flame of a stovetop or visit a doctor when we're injured. Pain hurts. We want pain to stop.

But avoiding pain is not always the best way of coping. We would never ignore a severe burn, yet when we feel the pain of a relationship ending, or the sting of loneliness, we tend to force our emotions behind a door, close it and then stand guard in front of it, hoping our feelings don't seep through the cracks.

There are consequences to our avoidance: we create patterns of behaviour in order to cope with our pain but end up being controlled by them. We distract ourselves from pain by keeping busy and wonder why we can't relax. We reach for our phones at every spare moment for a mindless scroll, because it's easier than being alone with our thoughts – and yet we feel disconnected and agitated. We bottle our emotions only to wind up at after-work drinks crying hysterically to Susan from Finance.

As a psychologist, I commonly observe in my clients the result of our tendencies to avoid pain: anxiety, depression, confusion, lack of direction and relationship issues. They find that they can't 'stop thinking' or control behaviours such as overworking, emotional eating or excessive alcohol consumption. They struggle with knowing what they want from life. They find it difficult to communicate and set boundaries. And quite often they are unaware that the challenges they come to therapy with are caused by their avoidance of uncomfortable feelings and an unwillingness to face painful past experiences.

When life gets messy, it is easy for us to struggle with our 'darkness'. Our darkness is represented by the parts of ourselves that we are afraid to show others. It is the feelings that keep us up at night, our insecurities and the times in our lives when nothing seems right. It's the times when we feel lost, disconnected and unsure of the path ahead.

We all have darkness in our lives. No matter how accomplished, successful, creative or self-aware we are, how much we earn, or how many followers we have, at some point, we all meet the scary corners of our minds. Even those who we believe have transcended suffering – spiritual teachers like the Dalai Lama, for example – grapple with pain.

The pain that we feel in our lives is often a very normal response to something going wrong, yet we tend to react to this pain with a sense of shame. We pretend to be happy when we are suffering inside and wear masks to protect our vulnerabilities: 'Everything is fine!' we claim – even in the throes of a meltdown. We find it hard to be honest about the shit that hurts us.

Your anxieties aren't there to be banished. Neither are the memories that haunt you, the sadness in your heart, the confusion that you might have about your future, your fears that you are not enough. And yet we treat these anxieties as outcasts, hiding in the corner of the playground eating a limp cold sandwich while we swing from handlebar to handlebar, pretending they don't exist.

The denial of our darkness actually covers up our 'humanness' – the very fabric that connects us all through this journey of life. Denying what we all feel prevents us from opening our hearts and being real and authentic. It closes us to life and possibilities.

The scariest thought in the world is that someday I'll wake up and realize I've been sleepwalking through my life: under-appreciating the people I love, making the same hurtful mistakes over and over, a slave to neuroses, fear, and the habitual.

To sleepwalk through life is to live controlled by your darkness, blindfolded and held back from possibility and numb to connection. Whether your darkness is seemingly invisible or rears its head daily, this is your chance to face it and wake up.

In the following pages, I will show you how to confront the darkness you have been carrying with you. I will guide you in identifying what is holding you back from moving forward, how to be with intense emotions and the scars of past hurts, and how to create space in your life for what really matters. The way I see it, we can spend all our time and energy trying to run away from our darkness or we can honour and respect it. We can learn to dance with the darkness.

***

I'm no stranger to darkness in my own life. I remember wondering in my early 20s why I had such 'bad luck' in relationships, and why I wasn't 'where I should be'. Friends around me seemingly transitioned into stable jobs and had a five-year plan, while I was still recklessly partying, doing drugs and 'going nowhere'.

I didn't like myself. I used to stand in front of the mirror and point out every flaw that I thought I had, and be so racked with disgust that I didn't want to leave the house. Afraid to be alone with my thoughts, I'd leave the TV on all night blaring infomercials and then berate myself for not being able to make it to my university classes. I dated people who had no respect for me and found flaws in everyone who was kind. It's hard to admit but there have been times I've hated myself and been consumed by anxiety and insecurity – and to be honest, I still battle with these monsters in my head.

It was only when I started studying psychology and found books that spoke to me that I realised my experience in the world was hugely influenced by my self-talk and the core belief that I was 'not good enough' – beliefs I wasn't even aware of holding. I found a mentor, a Buddhist monk and psychologist, who taught me how to develop my self-awareness, and I discovered that I wasn't speaking to myself very kindly. In fact, I was a bit of an asshole to myself.

But as it goes when you start a path of self-inquiry, I realised that there was so much to face – that learning to 'love myself' was not as easy as I thought. I've faced loss in my life. I've drowned in loneliness, despite being surrounded by people. And it took a deep dive into the unopened doors of my past to understand how to value myself. It's taken many reminders that my worth is not defined by my output of work, accomplishments, appearance or how much I could 'save' the world.

My journey is still unfolding, with undulating waves of growth and contraction, joy and despair – but in many ways, my darkness has been the light for others. Having been self-destructive, wild and a 'black sheep' helped me connect with people as I began work as a psychologist.

I started my career working with street kids for the Salvation Army's Oasis Youth Support Network, an inner-city crisis accommodation service that housed up to 13 homeless and disadvantaged young people each night aged between 16 and 21. Oasis gave young people access to programs and services to assist them to find stable housing, jobs and mental health support. Many of these young people had experienced severe and repeated trauma, mental health issues, and drug or alcohol addiction. They found it hard to trust people, and rightly so: many of them had been neglected by their parents or carers. They had protective walls to shield themselves from possible dangers – that often became barriers to positive and well-meaning influences too.

Let's just say that the street kids I was working with weren't always keen on coming to therapy ... or getting along with staff at the centre. Many of them preferred to smoke bongs in the nearby park than sit with me in the therapy room. There were incidents like fights among residents, abuse hurled, and the occasional chair would go flying at a staff member's head. Other psychologists and support workers came and went but I stayed, committed to finding a way to connect with these kids.

I had to learn pretty fast that it wasn't going to work if I was going to act like a 'know-it-all' authority figure. It helped that I could see myself in each person I worked with – I'd grown up hanging with Chinatown gangs and abused drugs and alcohol as a teenager. I didn't fit in at school and knew what it was to feel like an outcast. I knew how easy it was to turn to drugs, to get caught in the cycle of self-harm and to feel as though nobody was there for you. But most importantly, I scored brownie points for knowing who Tupac and Snoop were.

My manager at the time, a senior psychologist, Michelle, taught me about the quality of *transparency* as a psychologist, the ability to be okay with not having all the answers, and fostered the skill of allowing parts of *myself* to shine through to connect. By allowing me to be who I was, she enabled me to step outside the rigid bounds of what I thought a psychologist had to be to be successful – I didn't have to be perfect.

Thinking creatively was key: instead of trying to exude enthusiasm about the benefits of therapy to entice the kids into the room, I'd hold hip-hop, graffiti, surfing, DJ-ing and songwriting workshops, and let an authentic connection manifest through discussions of music, art, life on the streets and a down-to-earth approach to the issues that affected us all.

The messiness of being human is powerful – it connects us to each other because, at the heart of it, we're all rowing in the same shit-soup at times. We have the capacity to hurt others, and ourselves. We are all vulnerable, whether we like to admit it or not. We all have the same mystery of life presented to us. Remembering that we're in the same mix of magic and conundrum can keep us united. If only we could put down our masks, we could see that our struggles are one and the same: we all feel pain and desire joy, we all suffer, and we're all in this together.

Expressing and normalising these challenges isn't just beneficial for street kids but for us all. We don't have to have a mental health disorder to find life hard. It just is. We don't have to come from broken homes or have parents that are drug addicts to have trauma in our lives.

***

This 'collective messiness' of humans is one of the reasons why I started The Indigo Project. I've long felt that there were people falling through the cracks – those who just didn't align to traditional therapy, those who had been and hated it, and those who didn't want to focus on their problems in lieu of discovering their potential. I wanted to create a place in Sydney for adults that brought the same essence of the space I had created for my clients at the beginning of my career, when I worked with street kids for the Salvation Army. I wanted to bring what I'd learnt about injecting more 'human-ness', creativity and authenticity into the field of mental health.

Therapy doesn't have to be clinical or pretentious or exclusively for people with mental health disorders – it's about connection and relating in ways that normalise the journey through darkness. Dealing with your mental health has often been seen as an insular, private activity. But I think the opposite – community plays a huge role in your mental health. We can't go through the darkness alone.

Thinking creatively about mental health led me to experiment with community courses and events at Indigo that allowed people to show up, be vulnerable and have fun while exploring their minds. The flagship course, 'Get Your Shit Together', appealed to many – it included life skills like setting personal boundaries, dealing with stress, and techniques to develop self-awareness and self-acceptance. People told me it resonated because it taught them all the tools they were never shown when growing up. It normalised their challenges rather than making them feel as though they had problems, or were 'broken'.

I weaved music into our community offerings. *Listen Up* is a popular event where each month 60 people lie in a candle-lit room for a 'contemporary sound bath' – an experimental music experience where participants are guided through an album (by artists like Sigur Ros, Nils Frahm, Nicolas Jaar) or taken through a 'sound journey' that we create. *Listen Up* became a safe environment where people could explore their thoughts and emotions, and with surprising results – people often asked us if we had 'spiked their drinks', having experienced powerful, colourful, and cathartic journeys. Some people likened them to psychedelic drug experiences that helped them to connect emotionally, resolve concerns and feel connected and energised. Since starting

Listen Up, we've run the experience for Spotify, Facebook, and even thousands of school children at two separate music festivals – no matter the age, music has a way of connecting us to our emotions like nothing else.

Music has become a central component to my therapeutic approach. In recent years, I've designed immersive art installations that fuse the power of music with deep psychological processes to help people access and process feelings around topics such as death, fear and forgiveness. This inspired the audio experiences you will be introduced to throughout the book.

***

It means a lot to me that the clients who come to Indigo are so proud of seeing a therapist that they often tell their friends or mention it on social media. This kind of thing never used to be the norm. It has shown me that therapy and 'working on yourself' does not have to be something that you hide, something you're ashamed of – but a symbol of a desire for self-knowledge and courage.

Being a therapist has brought me great insight into what it means to be human, *and how similar we all are, at the end of the day.* I can't tell you how often I hear the words, 'Something's missing' or 'I just don't feel like I'm doing this right' in the therapy room – we all think that everyone is 'doing life' better than we are and that we've somehow missed the important memos.

There comes a time when we want more from life. We want to be in it, connected to it, and not just smashed around as though life's a dumping wave at the beach that's constantly threatening to rip off our bathers. We want to love with our whole hearts and not sweat so much of the small stuff. We want change. We all know change can be painful, but there comes a time when we feel the pain of not changing, and eventually it feels worse. It is in these moments that we often step into the unknown. Perhaps that is what brought you to this book – you are ready for change. There's a part of you that believes that you can meet your darkness and transform yourself. And you can.

You are capable of change. We all are. You have all the tools within yourself to evolve and grow in ways that you never thought were possible, sometimes by doing the opposite of what you've been thinking is right all these years. Trust me, you're about to see how the mind can be an incredible trickster – convincing you that people can't be trusted or that life is never going to get any better. You're about to discover that you are often acting in ways that you seemingly can't control because *something else within you* is actually pulling the strings – your subconscious mind. You are about to unravel who you really are beneath those layers of expectations and 'shoulds' that you are buried under.

Facing your darkness is really about facing yourself – and discovering that that person is someone worth loving, listening to and developing a solid relationship with. And this is key – you *can* form relationships with the parts of you that trouble, annoy or upset you. You don't need to banish the frustrating feelings, such as insecurity, anxiety, loneliness – you can learn how to see them in a different light.

There is abundant evidence of our ability to transform through tragedy and adversity – I see it in my clients every day. They don't have superpowers; in fact, they aren't much different from you or me. These people have healed from break-ups, recovered from broken hearts, carved out dreams for themselves, let go of past pain and found self-love. Through therapy and introspection, they develop self-respect, learn to set boundaries, communicate their needs, and find their capacity for compassion. They have learnt to explore their darkness, developing self-awareness and self-acceptance, growing into stronger and more resilient people.

We're here to shine our light on this process of personal transformation. I've dug into the research and my experience as a therapist to share *what works;* I've taken the guesswork out for you by laying out the tools and techniques that I have gathered and refined to help my clients over the last ten years.

***

Have you ever tried out a recipe only to have it look an absolute car crash in the end? Whenever that's happened to me, I've always wished I'd had the chef by my side, to help me through the steps and give me an idea of where we're going. Through this journey, I'll be sharing my recipes with you. But I'll be supporting you as you bring them to life. The final product will be different for everyone – after all, you'll be bringing many of your own ingredients, and it will be important that we tweak things to your taste. But this is what a strong self-development path should look like: you have a vague idea of where you are going, you take on the advice, but you also experiment with what works for you. And most importantly – you're never going to be alone.

There's only so much that words on a page can teach us. The self-help industry tends to tell people what to do, without explaining how to do it. They espouse maxims such as: Love yourself! Forgive others! Let go! Take action! Find your values! Feel your emotions! If it were that simple, we'd all have done it by now. As with my clients, I want to give you the *how* as well as the *what,* to unfold the journey with you, walking alongside you as you find yourself back home – to a place of connection within yourself, with the lights turned on.

Over the years I've developed structured exercises that will assist you in breaking down and absorbing new concepts. I recommend grabbing yourself a journal as you'll be getting hands-on with written reflections, meditations, playlists and audio experiences called 'sonic embodiments'.

What is a 'sonic embodiment'? I've spent the past four years developing this bespoke format of audio experiences, which combines music and psychological processes to help immerse you in this deep personal work, through beautiful instrumental music and meditation-like guidance. Sonic embodiments are a culmination of my research and practice. I have also worked with Dr Amanda Krause, a music psychologist, to further understand and refine this type of audio experience. Our research has shown how these audio experiences can promote real catharsis and people's emotional processing. We all know the power of music to heal; combined with audio guidance and the principles of somatic psychotherapy, it's a way of fully absorbing yourself in the work we're doing that can enhance the emotional shifts required for deep change. The music you will hear throughout these experiences has all been specially created for you by composer Rich Lucano (Phondupe). I've also curated a ten-hour playlist of music to accompany and enhance your experience of reading this book – I want you to feel completely immersed and held while in the dark.

This is a big process. Dealing with your darkness is more involved than self-care and bubble baths. It is the creation of the moving, living, dynamic artwork that you are, a conscious remembering and honouring of the wisdom you have always held. This is about enduring, lasting, sacred and profound transformation, the shedding of old skins, a human metamorphosis. For the next 200 pages or so, we are on this journey together.

***

We are journeying hand in hand in more ways that you might think – while writing this book I could have never anticipated that my path would mirror yours and that I would find myself in the dark. In November 2017, two weeks after the first discussion with my publisher about this book, my father passed away. Life was already on a knife's edge with the stress of his illness and juggling the demands of The Indigo Project, which was under a lot of financial stress. Adding grief to the mix was complicated. Grieving while writing a book on top of the pressure I was putting on myself to 'get it right' and 'be perfect' led to a severe emotional and mental breakdown.

I felt as though something inside of me had snapped, but in reality my breakdown was not because of one thing but the load that I had unwittingly carried for many years. In simple terms, I wasn't giving *myself* the attention I deserved. I had let my need for validation, and an unhealthy habit of putting other people first, rule my life. My therapist would say: 'You left yourself.'

'Leaving yourself' is when you put everyone and everything else before yourself. I discovered it was an old pattern of mine, but also one that I have helped many of my clients work with. I found myself taking my own medicine, on an *Inception* -like journey: a therapist in therapy writing about therapy ... life imitating art, and vice versa. It was a process that required me to go deep, back into my past, revisiting old wounds, early childhood experiences and facing unmet grief. It was a huge wake-up call: I was tested in my practice of vulnerability. I had to learn how to ask for help, to lean on others, to accept uncertainty. I had to sit with uncomfortable feelings, learn how to be kind to myself and figure out what was really important to me.

In no small words, writing this book has seen my 'rebirth' and the death of my old identity. It's strange, but I feel more 'me' than I have in years: I'm rekindling old friendships that I had lost, able to lose myself in conversations instead of being gripped by anxiety or feelings of disconnection. I trust much more than I ever have that everything is going to be okay – and that running around like a headless chook, saying yes to everyone's demands and filling my day with meeting other people's expectations isn't the way to a healthy, sustainable lifestyle.

I believe in this process you are embarking on, not only because I have seen it change my clients' lives but my own. I mean it when I say, *I am with you.*

***

In your hands are a set of bronzed keys. These are the keys to the self-knowledge, emotional freedom and connection that you have been longing for. They open the door to your darkness, and in that darkness lies the gold of transformation and self-discovery.

It's time to step into the dark.

CHAPTER 1

The Light in the Haunted House

Why Your Answers Lie in Your Shadows

Imagine this: you are standing in front of an old haunted mansion, the doorknob is covered in moss and cobwebs. This house represents the parts of you that you typically avoid: your fears, insecurities and painful memories – this is your darkness. You shiver, knowing that you need to step into this eerie, creepy house, feeling the pull of its energy. You can hear the distant cackling and growling of the creatures inside and you feel a pit of anxiety in your belly. Something in your heart tells you that it's important to step into this house, to face the things that trouble you. That somewhere in the darkness of this house lie the answers you've been looking for. Clues that may help you find peace, love and connection within yourself, and a life authentic to you.

Most of us tend to conjure up a similar image in our minds when imagining a haunted house: a ramshackle, beaten-up structure, with wild overgrown gardens, broken windows and an air of treachery and abandonment surrounding the building. Seemingly haunted by spirits, it's a place few of us would ever dare venture into.

When I became a psychologist, sitting with clients and their stories of hurt and disappointment, I started to recognise that the haunted house lives *within us.* I started to see my therapy room as a portal to these haunted houses, a safe space where my clients could explore the inner worlds that they once feared. A place where they could be with the parts of their lives they are most afraid of: where the monsters, skeletons and spirits in their minds could come out to play.

In therapy, we hold the knobbly hands of skeletons and peer into their hollowed eyes. We give the spirits names and a voice to speak with. We flush out the monsters under the bed and tango with them. It is in these experiences with the dark that my clients discover themselves for who they really are: brave, courageous, creative and insightful selves, holding the light of wisdom, bright and strong.

Through this book, you now have a portal to the haunted house within you too. You can open the door to a deeper understanding of who you are, what you need to thrive and what makes life worth living. By opening this book you have taken the first step.

Before you place your hand on the doorknob, let's get prepared. Like with any journey, you'll want to feel equipped. In this chapter we're going to do the groundwork; let's answer the question of why you are here, what you want to get out of this, and what you might expect from the transformational process. I want you to hear about those who have ventured into the murky unknown and understand the science of post-traumatic growth – bound to give you perspective on the wisdom hidden in your life challenges. This is unexplored territory. To help you on your way, I'll supply you with a backpack full of tools, and you'll be ready to take your first steps.

Finding light in the dark

I once visited an experimental installation – *Backside of the Moon,* by American artist James Turrell – in Naoshima, Japan, in a building by architect Tadao Ando. Turrell is most recognised for his work on light and its impact on spatial perception. To enter, I had to drag my hand against a wall, in complete darkness, using it to feel my way into the house. Through a maze of corners, I felt a seat in front of me. I sat down. It was pitch-black and disorientating. Things looked the same, whether I opened or closed my eyes. I felt a little fear creep in.

I sat there for ten minutes, wondering what the point of it all was, and silently freaking out. I wanted to escape from the depth of the dark unknown. After a while, I noticed a small light in the distance. Slowly it grew bigger and bigger, and over the course of twenty minutes, it formed what seemed like a faint glowing rectangle. I gradually started to notice the outline of other people in the room, and at this point, a voice in the room invited us to assess the rectangle. I gingerly walked towards the light and tried to touch it, thinking there would be a wall, an object or a projection, but when I got there, there was no wall. It was an empty void. It was bizarre. The light in the room hadn't 'slowly appeared' after ten minutes, it had *always been there.* It was not as if the light had been turned up or down – this was a clever manipulation of my perception. What I once saw as darkness, was actually light, but my eyes had to adjust in order to see it. I was so convinced that the light 'had appeared', and yet it had always been there.

The light that was 'always there' in my experience of James Turrell's installation reminds us that things aren't always as they seem – even darkness itself is a perception, a shade of light.

So, what if there was a chance that *your* darkness contained light? What if your painful, tormenting and at times unbearable experiences could fundamentally change you for the better? What if these aversive experiences were crucial in helping you transform and transition into the next evolution of yourself – someone more in touch with themselves, aligned to their hopes and dreams, a person with purpose in this world?

When it comes to transformation through adversity, science has a resounding opinion.

We are stronger than we think

It's when we feel we have nothing left to give, to offer, to resurrect that the paradox of transformation through adversity is within our grasp.

Throughout history we have been reminded of this strength and urged to look beyond our wounds, and the times we've fallen into unfavourable situations, towards the wisdom that could exist in its wake. The German philosopher Friedrich Nietzsche summed it up with the words, 'That which doesn't kill us makes us stronger', a sentiment echoed by Kelly Clarkson, Kanye West, and me circa 3am at the karaoke bar.

These musings aren't just the trumpet of philosophers and musicians but also of researchers in recent years, demonstrating how *we can grow through pain and challenge.* Even in the case of severe stress and trauma, in situations where most of us would think, *I would not survive that* – the death of someone you love, finding out you have a terminal disease, being assaulted – studies are finding that people aren't just resilient, or finding a way to 'bounce back', but that they are transforming into stronger, more cohesive versions of themselves, with a clearer view on life.

In 2004, researchers Alex Linley and Stephen Joseph reviewed studies that documented positive changes in people dealing with various forms of trauma (such as breast cancer, chronic illness, and military combat), finding that as many as 70% of survivors reported positive change in at least one area in life, including changes in outlook on life, social connections and how they perceived themselves.

Researchers Rebecca Collins, Shelley Taylor and Laurie Skokan from the University of California spoke to cancer patients following their diagnosis, finding that individuals reported more positive changes than negative, with shifts in their views on themselves, priorities, plans for the future and perspective on the world. Researcher Steven Schwartzberg conducted intensive clinical interviews with HIV-positive men into the effect their diagnosis had on their sense of meaning. He found that 74% of the individuals reported that their HIV infection led to positive mental changes. The words of this participant really struck a chord with me:

'This is it, you know, moment to moment, and trying to enjoy it, every moment. I'm not always successful, but I feel – not quite a pressure, but a strong sense that this is the only time we have, not next week, but now. Get everything you can out of living: do what you want to do, enjoy it. This feels like a positive thing, not a desperate thing – trying to treasure what's happening right now.'

Psychologists Richard Tedeschi and Lawrence Calhoun from the University of North Carolina, Charlotte, coined the term *post-traumatic growth* to represent this phenomenon, defining it as the 'positive psychological change experienced as a result of the struggle with highly challenging life circumstances'. 'Experiencing growth in the wake of trauma,' Tedeschi states, 'is far more common than P.T.S.D.'

Their research studied psychological changes in people who had experienced adversity such as the death of a loved one, surviving a natural disaster and overcoming a major illness – and uncovered five major shifts: 'greater appreciation of life and changed sense of priorities; warmer, more intimate relationships with others; a greater sense of personal strength; recognition of new possibilities or paths for one's life; and spiritual development'.

Of course, these positive changes don't happen straight away. Highly stressful circumstances initially cause distress, such as anxiety, sadness or depression, but Tedeschi and Calhoun found that managing these disturbances led to positive changes. More specifically, highly stressful events and circumstances cause us to re-examine our core beliefs: our beliefs about the world we live in, ourselves and other people. According to Tedeschi and Calhoun, growth and transformation involve rebuilding positive self-beliefs and a view of the world that takes into account the changed reality of how a person's life has changed.

They liken this process to the reconstruction of buildings after an earthquake so that they are more 'resistant to being shattered'. The degree to which the traumatic event challenges core beliefs has been shown to be a key element in making the experience of post-traumatic growth possible. The greater the person felt the need to re-examine their core beliefs, the higher the likelihood they would experience growth.

According to Tedeschi and Calhoun's model for post-traumatic growth, life challenges create opportunities for individuals to dive into the darkness of their haunted house and come out with new perspectives: to confront their limiting beliefs, manage their difficult feelings and create meaning from adversity.

But let's pause a moment here. Perhaps you are thinking: 'But I haven't experienced the type of adversity that this research is studying. I'm experiencing anxiety/confusion/a break-up. Do I have to have experienced this level of trauma to experience the benefits of transformation and growth?' The answer is no – all types of darkness bring the opportunity for positive change.

Take my client, 'Kate'. She is hard-working and motivated, working day and night to transition from her corporate role in events management into a side-business as a retreat creator and facilitator. She came to therapy because she was experiencing intense anxiety and insecurity, concerned that she 'didn't know enough' to be a successful business owner. She built elaborate business plans and even volunteered on other retreats to get more experience but always felt she was a fake.

I often work with clients who want to transition out of their 'safe' jobs into vocations that they are passionate about. At the core of their darkness is imposter syndrome, the belief that they will be 'found out' for being a 'fraud'. Many clients also have fears around leaving a stable income or of failure. Working with Kate on her anxiety led us down the path of understanding where her core beliefs that she was 'a fraud' or needed security came from. We discovered that financial security was a pain point for her because her family had been disadvantaged growing up, and her father always yelled at her if she spent money on herself. Her imposter syndrome formed from high school, where she attended an academic school. There she was bullied and always felt inferior to her classmates.

Working through these experiences at the core of her anxieties was hard – Kate had to revisit uncomfortable feelings that were buried and face memories of painful situations from her childhood. But in doing so, she transformed. She learnt how to instil a new belief system that shifted her whole perspective on not only her ability as a facilitator and business owner but in her personal relationships. She became more open with her friends and more confident. She built a successful retreat business and feels grateful that she confronted her fears and anxieties. It changed her life.

The majority of my clients have not experienced severe trauma but nevertheless have difficulties that, with work, give rise to clarity in life direction, healthier relationships and self-knowledge. They find their resilience much like the research participants who experienced post-traumatic growth. These people are the new parents who feel challenged by their 'loss of freedom', the person who struggles to find love, the people who get lost in feelings of disconnection and loneliness from their busy lifestyles. They are you. They are me.

Facing your fears

It's normal to have some fears or reservations about exploring your darkness. You might think that you've tried everything or that you can't change. You might be afraid of what you'll find, or fear feeling overwhelmed. Let's be real – the thought of embracing the not-so-great moments in our lives is enough to make most people want to run for the hills.

Wouldn't it be great if we didn't have to grapple with guilt, loneliness and fear? How different our lives would be if *that thing* didn't happen – that failure, that disaster, that crushing loss? Why does the past have to regurgitate itself in our lives? Why would anyone in their right mind want to confront their painful memories and fears? I know, I know – I also think these things.

Just remember that inside us all is a little child who is afraid of the dark. We all have a snotty, scared younger self who wants to hide under the covers and sleep with the light on, afraid of the monsters under the bed and the creatures of the night. It is this part of us that is terrified of venturing into our darkness, our imagination in overdrive, guessing at what might lie in the shadows.

There is good reason why this fear is deeply ingrained – it kept us alive. From an evolutionary perspective, a primal urge to see the light as good and safe, and the dark as dangerous and scary, makes sense. The night held the possibility of predators, the possibility of death. For our ancestors, light equalled *life:* fire provided a source of warmth, protection from wild animals and a tool to navigate the dark forest paths. The impetus to seek the light has not left us.

Even though everything in our bodies tells us to run away, in order to treat a fear, we often must face it. This principle underlies *exposure therapy* – a technique in which therapists introduce clients to their fear through small repeated exposures, gradually building their capacity to become less reactive. We unknowingly practise exposure therapy on ourselves; think about the times you prepared for a presentation for school or work. You may have practised in front of a mirror or with a friend, building awareness around the distressing thoughts and emotions triggered by your fear of public speaking. You may have noticed that your palms get sweaty or that your heart beats faster – but realise that these are physiological symptoms that you can be aware of. You may notice thoughts such as 'I can't do this', or 'Everyone thinks I'm an idiot', but learn how to acknowledge them without letting them overwhelm you. With repeated practices, or 'exposures', you are learning to 'be with' and accept the fear, which enables you to stand up in front of your peers and present with confidence.

Similarly, you are facing your fears of your own darkness by exposing yourself to them through this journey, opening yourself to them little by little. You will get nervous, sweaty, and feel like running away at times – but you can learn to accept these reactions.

What you do not face, you cannot deal with. Ignoring your shitty relationship will not make it better. Sucking it up at the job you hate won't make it more enjoyable. Accepting bullshit from your friends is not going to stop their behaviour. You can't wish your worries away. But you can shine a light on them.

The transformational process

If I had a dollar for every time I could sense that someone in my therapy room wanted a quick solution to their problems in a single session, I would have retired by now. A transformational process is a series of changes that effectively evolves who you are at the core. It is complex, at times challenging and takes patience.

This is how I see it: if it were that easy to drive in a straight line from attachment to detachment, from anxiety to calmness, from resentment to forgiveness, we'd all do it – but it's not. To transform your mind and life, you are going to need tools, guidance and instructions on where you're going and what to expect. You probably wouldn't set out for a week-long hike without a backpack of food, shelter and a map – so how could you delve into the complexity of the human mind without the faintest idea of the terrain?

From a higher level perspective, how you transition, change and transform must take into account an array of puzzle pieces: how the brain works, our evolutionary adaptations, the effect of the subconscious, and the influence of our environments.

Given the complexity of the human mind and its idiosyncrasies, we need multilayered processes that can target issues holistically – or in simpler terms, we have to hit this thing from all angles. It takes more than willpower to change – the mind needs to be trained, respected and understood. We need to develop self-awareness, self-acceptance, patience and self-compassion to love ourselves. We have to understand our needs, boundaries and style of communication to have healthy relationships. We need to find forgiveness in our hearts to heal and let go. We need creativity and community to find purpose and meaning. And we must surrender to the unknown to instil awe and wonder within us. The good news is: this is what lies ahead for you.

This transformation involves identifying the root causes of why you think, feel and behave the way you do, in order to fundamentally shift your perspective on life. By doing this, you can experience an 'identity shift', where your true values and needs become so apparent, you can consciously make decisions for your life path, harbouring what is meaningful to you.

The chapters ahead will take you through the different 'rooms' of your haunted house and the types of 'darkness' they hold. In each room of your house, you will be meeting the creatures that you might typically avoid, such as the 'monsters' in your mind and the 'skeletons' of past memories, discovering how to learn from them. We will develop your inner wisdom, uncover the roots of your patterns and help you understand all the parts of yourself.

Transformation is a process: that is, one learning or action will lead to another. It is designed at times to be challenging, so stick with it and come back to your intentions if you need to. I ask that you give yourself ample space and time to work through the experiences in order to fully immerse yourself in them and have time for self-reflection and integration. This is how you will get the best out of this journey. Remember that you aren't just 'solving a problem' but overhauling and enacting a deep spring-clean on your life.

Transformation is complex – so if this all sounds 'heady' and confusing as I outline it, I totally understand. For example, you might wonder what self-worth, self-acceptance, self-compassion and all the 'self-help' lingo even means – and what does it look like when you actually have 'achieved' these things? The simple answer is that these words are different ways of helping you to *find connection within yourself.*

Throughout this book, you will find that 'connection with yourself' can be explored through: self-awareness (how do you see all the parts of yourself clearly?), self-acceptance (how do you accept all the parts of you, as you are?), wisdom (how do you find and trust your inner voice?) self-compassion (how do you treat yourself with kindness?), self-care (how do you look after your needs?), self-worth (how do you value yourself?), breaking your patterns (how do you rewire your habits and make space for possibility?), authenticity (how do you live the life you want?) and appreciation of life (how can you be grateful for what you already have?).

Underpinning many of my teachings will be the *role of the body* in transformation and healing. While you may think a therapist's work is all about the mind, the body plays a crucial role in the expression and processing of emotions and trauma, and it will be a vital instrument in gaining more connection with yourself. For those interested in the science, other therapeutic modalities in this book are: somatic psychotherapy, emotion-focused therapy, mindfulness, parts work and positive psychology.

***

I want you to take a moment to notice something by your feet – it's a backpack filled with tools to help you on this journey. There's your phone, so you can always call a friend if you feel stuck or overwhelmed. I encourage you to use this lifeline, and to use it as much as you can. Know that I will always be around too while you move through the shadows. On this phone, you will also be able to access the meditations and audio experiences that have been created to help you on your way. Put on your headphones and the warm coat I've brought along for you.

The most important tool you'll need is your torch, but you'll soon discover this is something that you already own.

This journey packs a punch. You'll be getting your hands dirty. But soon, that haunted house of yours will be tidied, renovated and liveable – not something you avoid.

How are you, really?

It's crucial that you get a sense of what your motivation is to be here, but sometimes it can be hard to articulate. Before we dive into your intentions for your journey, it may help you to understand some of my work as a therapist and the reasons why people come to therapy, so you can get clear on yours.

Most assume that my work as a psychologist is with clients who are severely traumatised or have mental health conditions, those at their wits' end. When I divulge my vocation to others, people are often in disbelief that I can 'subject' myself day in and day out to the difficulties and darkness of people's lives – 'I could never do that' people regularly comment. If you imagine that I'm only dealing with the shitty bits of a person's life – that my couch only holds the weight of complex traumas, disorders, and dysfunction – it does paint a very grim picture of therapy and the people within its walls.

It's hard not to perceive the 'dark side' of the human mind as negative – we only have to glance at the news to view harrowing stories of people who perform unspeakable atrocities, to see the celebrities who have 'lost their minds', or witness film characters like the Joker or Darth Vader – deeply tortured souls with insurmountable neuroses.

As a psychologist, I get to observe the slivers of people's lives that lie behind closed doors and hidden deep within our psyches. On the whole, all of us have a lot of the same quirks – we worry a lot about what other people think of us, we want to find genuine love and connection and, generally, most of us are confused about how to do this whole life thing.

I see people in times of struggle, in times of transition, crisis and change. It is at these times – when they are tied up in emotional challenges of relationships not going right, in workplaces that are demanding, in grief and loss – that people can't see the path clearly before them. I see people bound by their restrictive or *self-limiting beliefs* about themselves. (*I'm not good enough, I am not worthy of love, I will never be successful, I don't know what I want.*)

Our struggles come from our desire to want things differently than how they are: we're on a constant treadmill of 'doing' because we don't think we have, or are, enough.

The acceptance of *what is* is hard. It is painful for us when things don't go our way, and when we struggle to accept who we are, when we play games and have power struggles in relationships, when we fear being vulnerable. Experiencing challenges, no matter how much the change is needed, is painful.

Many of us are 'do-ers', on an endless quest for achievement, autonomy and individuality, but tend to get left feeling burnt out and behind the 8-ball. We chase the proverbial carrot of 'having it all' and whip ourselves for not 'doing enough' – we are the jockey *and the* horse in the never-ending race for fulfilment and satisfaction.

The reality is people come to therapy for a variety of reasons and not all of them are obvious at the outset. Sometimes, it's the unexpected that motivates people: going through a break-up, getting injured, getting fired from a job, a business failing or losing a loved one. Sometimes, it's a bushfire – or even a pandemic.

Most commonly, I see clients grappling with symptoms of stress, anxiety, depression and unresolved trauma showing up as patterns of behaviour that they can't control: addiction, overworking, overextending for others or aggressiveness. At times, people tell me that they just feel 'lost', 'disconnected' or 'stuck', despite having perfectly functional lives with jobs, relationships and stable environments.

While I see people for a wide variety of reasons, I've noticed we all ultimately have similar underlying questions: *Who am I? How do I stop worrying? How do I deal with my crazy thoughts? How do I have great relationships? How can I deal with my emotions? How do I let go of pain? What is my purpose in life?*

Take a moment to think about why you are here. Pause and contemplate what motivated you to pick up this book in the first place. Take your time; this part is important. If you're unsure, think about the parts of your life that you are satisfied with and not so satisfied with. What keeps you up at night? How are you feeling? What relationships aren't serving you? Have you experienced a difficulty that you are finding hard to get over? Do you recognise that there is something that you need to let go of to help you move forward?

To get started, we're going to assess where you're at in your life, what you are happy with and not so happy with – and where there are opportunities for change, transition and acceptance. We go directly to the areas that need attention; solving problems in our lives cannot be achieved by skirting around or steamrolling over them – we wouldn't fix a cut on our finger by bandaging our toe.

An assessment of your life is about making the time to take stock of how you're feeling and admitting if some things just aren't cutting it for you: that could include friends who bring you down, attitudes that hold you back or the belief that you're not worthy of love.

I'd like to ease you into this process by giving you two exercises to get you thinking. The objective is to be honest with yourself – you can't remedy what you won't admit is not working. It takes courage to be honest with where you're at. In doing so, you are taking *responsibility* for your life. It means you are getting in the driver's seat to steer it in the right direction, instead of letting it drift aimlessly.

Exercise 1: Holistic Scorecard

A holistic scorecard is an exercise designed to give you a clear assessment of the areas in your life. It is a way of acknowledging where you're at, and want to be, in different areas of your life.

Go through the areas of your life in the list one by one and in Column A rate how satisfied you are out of 10 (0 = not great, 10 = highly satisfied). In Column B, rate how well would you like to be doing in this area of your life out of 10.

As you go through the list of areas in your life, some of them will apply to you more than others. Remember that not every area in our lives has to be a 10 – in other words, check in with your perfectionistic tendencies! It's easy to feel the pressure to be perfect in all areas of our lives but the aim is to really get clear on the areas that you would like to transform. For example, maybe exercise is not a huge priority for you right now, and that's okay.

                                      A   B

1. Family   ____ ____
2. Friends   ____ ____
3. Romantic relationships   ____ ____
4. Exercise   ____ ____
5. Diet   ____ ____
6. Sleep   ____ ____
7. Work   ____ ____
8. Study/Learning   ____ ____
9. Creativity   ____ ____
10. Movement towards dreams and aspirations   ____ ____
11. Contribution to society/Giving back   ____ ____
12. Connection to community   ____ ____
13. Stress and anxiety management   ____ ____
14. Other _____   ____ ____

After you have finished the holistic scorecard, you will have a better idea about your intentions for this journey. You will be able to see the areas that are problematic for you, and others that you are content with. Notice which areas have the biggest discrepancy between Column A and

B. The larger the discrepancy, the more you want to work on this area.

Exercise 2: Your Intentions

Thinking about your intentions and what you would like to get out of the experience will help prepare you for the pathway ahead. Grab a journal or a blank piece of paper and record your answers. There are no right or wrong answers. A paragraph (3–6 sentences) will suffice for each question.

1. Why do you feel the need to take a transformational journey? What motivated you to open this book?

2. Are there particular issues that you would like to work on? For example, are there relationships that you would like to heal? Would you like to work on any unhealthy patterns or habits that you are noticing? How are you feeling?

3. What are your intentions for this experience? What do you want to get out of it?

> 4. What would make you feel more alive? What would you like to change? For example, if you refer back to an area that you would like to change in your holistic scorecard, what changes would allow you to move from, say, a 7 to an 8?
> 5. What has been the cost of not changing?
> 6. What are your fears or reservations about the journey ahead?

How did these exercises feel? Do you have a clearer picture of the parts of your life you want to transform?

Regardless of the source of your challenge, you have an opportunity for growth. Through adversity, you can come back to life – transforming your negative self-beliefs and unhelpful narratives about who you *think* you are. You can find space, possibility and direction – living the life that you want, having let go of the past. You can open your heart – becoming more forgiving, compassionate, and tap into a greater sense of belonging. Yes, getting to that point is a skill. And you're about to learn how to develop it.

This is a glimpse of your path. You will enter your haunted house, and within each room you will face a hidden aspect of yourself. The rooms may be cluttered, and you may find yourself falling over or getting frustrated with the dance. But this struggle will feed your growth, transformation and rebirth. You will find that all the things you are looking for – healing, connection, clarity and direction – are found in a place that you wouldn't typically look: within you.

You are not alone

And so here you are, standing silently in front of that old, musty mansion in your mind, drawing up the courage to take that first step across the threshold. You realise the sweaty key is in your palm but feel yourself wanting to pull away.

You aren't alone.

All I had to do is send one email. To my therapist. And ask for help.

Before I had my breakdown, I was choking with anxiety, I was scared. The little child within me was hiding under her blanket, in a place where she hoped no-one would find her. The monsters were out of control.

I felt ashamed that I was in this position, heading towards an emotional meltdown. I thought I 'should have known better'. I should have prevented it – considering that my job was to help people through their mental health challenges. I'm a psychologist. I lead a team of forty therapists. I'm writing a book about mental health – was this seriously happening to me?

I wrote the email to my therapist but it lay in my drafts folder, unsent for weeks. In my mind, I had 'things to do', I didn't have 'time' to have an appointment. In reality, I was scared of being vulnerable and terrified about what I would uncover.

I got on with life for a while, suffering silently, hoping that the overwhelming feelings of despair would go away. But it only got worse.

Although it's ideal to 'nip things in the bud', we often ignore our pain until things get really, really bad before we do something about them – myself included. The final straw came when I found myself Googling whether I had a heart condition, because the chest pains were so bad they were preventing me from sleeping. I was not having a heart attack – it was crippling anxiety. I was petrified that the stress I was putting myself under would lead to a disease like cancer. The cost of not changing was starting to outweigh the cost of doing nothing. I sent the email.

Throughout the therapeutic process, my anxiety did intensify sometimes, and I wanted to run away from the process. But every time those thoughts crept in, I reminded myself of the degree of pain I was in when I started, and remembered how much I didn't want to go back there. My journal entry with my intentions reminded me there was a cost to not changing, to remaining stuck.

Even when we know what is beneficial for us, we can resist it. We make excuses, pretend everything is okay, find flaws and think that we can do it by ourselves so we don't have to engage. We do everything we can to avoid meeting our pain.

But you can do this. You have the ability to walk through your darkness, to meet your pain and find your way out of it, to be recalibrated into something stronger. You will soon see the magic that happens when you light the candle within the walls of your own darkness and walk the unknown steps towards a greater understanding of yourself. You have the power to move mountains within you, to unravel the darker threads and transform them into something beautiful, meaningful and golden.

Take a deep breath, place the key in the moss-covered doorknob and push open the door.

CHAPTER 2

Monsters and Skeletons

What Makes You Think the Way You Do

Stepping inside, you take a breath of the musty, stale air. With the last of the evening light seeping through the dirty, broken windows, you begin to make out where you are standing: in a grand old lobby. Towards the back of the cavernous room is a majestic staircase lined with deep red carpet and stone balustrades. Ornate mirrors of different sizes cover almost all of the wall space. These mirrors are reflecting parts of you, reminding you that you are here to face yourself: you can see your muddied sneaker in one, the arch of your spine and your backpack in another, your darkened profile reflected further along.

At first, the only sound is your footsteps walking hesitantly across the creaking floorboards. 'Is anyone around?' you think to yourself. You start to hear familiar whispers: *I can't believe you're in your thirties and you don't have a stable job! You're going to be alone forever: forget getting married and having kids. You should lose some weight. Why are you such a loser? You will be hurt again.* You swivel around but see no-one, yet you can still hear scuttling, as if there are rats somewhere in the room.

You are in the lobby with your own negative self-beliefs and thoughts, and the scratching you can hear is the monsters in your head. To transform and grow, you need to meet them and discover where they have come from. This will lead you to the basement of your house, to meet the skeletons of your past. If only you had a torch, you could see what was hiding in the dark...

***

You have learnt from research in post-traumatic growth that examining and rebuilding your limiting beliefs plays a crucial role in transformation and growth. Now it's time for you to discover your own.

In this chapter, you will meet the monsters in your head and the skeletons of the past. They are powerful creatures, infiltrating every part of your life, from how you think, the decisions you make and the emotions you feel. You carry them around every day, taking on their whispers and influences.

Your monsters are your limiting beliefs, the critical, nasty and unhelpful thoughts that plague you, clouding your perspective. Your skeletons are the past experiences that birthed the monsters. Together, they have the capability to shape every aspect of your experience.

It might help you to imagine them this way: when watching a movie at the cinemas, the monsters are like the film, giving rise to what you see, hear and feel, whereas the skeletons are the makers of the film; you might never 'see' the creators but they are the invisible 'directors' of the whole movie.

And so, the question to you is this: are you going to let someone else direct the story of your life? The lead characters, the setting, the plot ... Or are you going to write it yourself? Chances are, you may have already tried. New Year's resolutions or health pacts are a perfect example of well-meaning attempts to transform that can fail to deal with the root cause of our problems. We've all heard the growl of the inner monster that snipes, 'You should really lose some weight.' Its words might be cast by a self-belief like, 'I am ugly.' The problem is that belief hides behind the advice it gives us. So, you follow its words and vow to 'get fit for the summer' on a Monday, only to find yourself at McDonalds at 1am the following weekend nursing twenty nuggets. And the pattern repeats. In these cases, we do everything to change our lives on the surface but fail to address the root causes of our habits. A healthier life might affect how we physically see ourselves, but will it shift a deep-seated self-loathing? I'm sorry to say that most the time, it won't. We have to transform from the inside out ... Meaningful change comes from an understanding of your core beliefs and the situations that gave rise to them.

When the directors change, the plot changes too.

The monsters

The monsters in your mind are tricksters. They come in different guises, such as *confirmation biases, negativity biases* and limiting self-beliefs. With their power to wield such a strong influence over your behaviours and emotions, it is important to get familiar with these unhelpful thoughts. First, let's understand the different types, and then their influence.

Types of monsters

A common monster is our confirmation bias. It shows up when we are *so sure of ourselves,* adamant that our perceptions are correct – and so we unconsciously choose to only see the things that reinforce our beliefs. Have you ever been so convinced about an issue, only to have something happen that instantly proves how off the mark you were? Maybe someone cuts you off in traffic – *What an arsehole. How could someone be such a prick?* Your anger starts to bubble up. *They obviously did it on purpose.* You speed up to give them a piece of your mind and flip them the bird ... and see an elderly lady who's struggling to hold the wheel. You start to calm down. It only takes a fleeting moment to realise how misguided you were in your thinking.

Meet the monster known as the worst case scenario, often experienced as: 'I don't know if this is going to last', 'I'm going to mess this up', or the ever-popular, 'I'll never find love.' This monster is a demonstration of negativity bias; that is, our tendency to give more weight to the negative aspects of a situation. These are the times we remember the things that went wrong – like when you walk out of a performance review stewing over that one piece of constructive feedback rather than acknowledging all the positive comments or when you only remember the bad dessert at an otherwise incredible dinner date.

Other monsters are expressed in habits such as overgeneralising, exaggerating, jumping to conclusions, playing the blame game or catastrophising: 'Why does this always happen to me?', 'I knew she would do this', 'I ruin everything', 'That's just the way it is.' Sound familiar?

The influence of monsters

The *cognitive triangle* – an illustration of the interconnectedness of our thoughts, feelings and behaviours – is a good starting point for understanding the influence of your monsters.

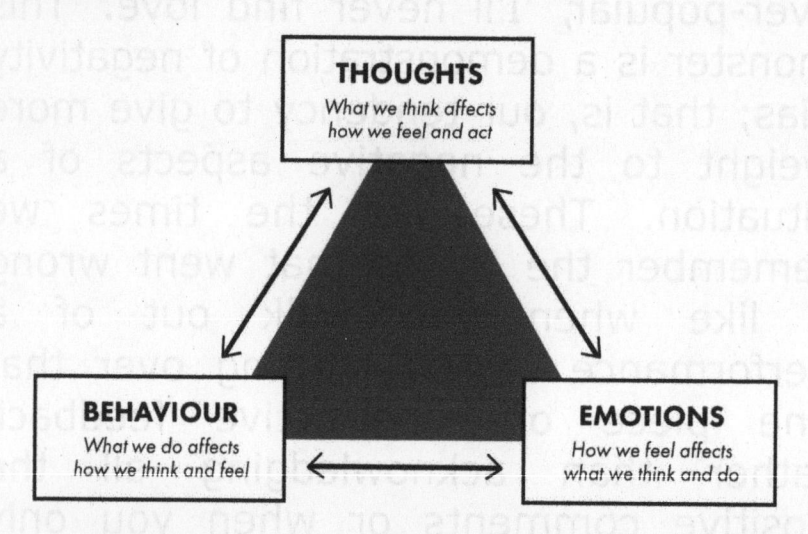

THOUGHTS
What we think affects how we feel and act

BEHAVIOUR
What we do affects how we think and feel

EMOTIONS
How we feel affects what we think and do

Let's say you believe the monsters in your head are telling you that people can't be trusted (thoughts/beliefs). You can find yourself avoiding dates or stopping yourself from becoming close to people (behaviours/actions), or perhaps feeling anxious or fearful (feelings/emotions). Or maybe you hold a belief that you will never be successful. You feel unconfident and insecure as a result of these thoughts. You talk yourself out of applying for a job that you really want because, deep down, you don't think you'll get it.

When these thoughts, feelings or behaviours are repeated, you see the creation of *patterns* or *habits* in your life. How often have you said to yourself: 'I *always* do this...' when something goes wrong? Or 'That's just the way I am.' This is a sign that there is a limiting self-belief doing its thing in the shadows while you take its dodgy opinion as fact.

Self-beliefs

Think about that for a moment. We all have thoughts about ourselves. Do you take yours as gospel, or do you question them? Most of us accept these thoughts without pulling back the curtains to reveal the invisible director that steers them. Let's walk you through how your belief system affects your whole life. Take your time to think about the answers to the questions I'm about to ask you. If it helps, grab your journal and pen for this section.

> *I'd like you to think about a moment that shaped your life. How old were you when this happened? What happened?*

Did you leave home, move overseas, end a relationship or get divorced? Perhaps you started a business or changed jobs or career, had a child, or fell ill. Perhaps someone close to you became incapacitated and you became a carer, or someone you love passed away. What makes these moments or phases in our lives 'life-changing' is the way they alter our belief systems, the lens through which we see the world. Think about it: if your life-changing moment was losing your dream job, your belief that you were a capable person could change to 'I will never be successful.' This has consequences on your feelings and reactions: you might not go for a new job that seems like a stretch. You might feel insecure and fearful. If you got your heart broken, your belief that you were worthy of love could change to 'I am unlovable.' You might find yourself avoiding relationships, or feeling depressed.

There are two types of beliefs – limiting and negative or expanding and positive. Positive self-belief can be: 'I am loved, I can trust others, I am a good person.' These beliefs open you up to life's possibilities and help you develop self-respect. Limiting self-beliefs can be: 'I am useless, I am not worthy of love, I am not capable.' These negative beliefs limit you as a person, keeping you closed off or hesitant to try new experiences. They are possibility-killers.

Thinking back to the experience that changed your life, how did your beliefs or values change during this time? What beliefs did you carry forward? Do these beliefs limit you or are they positive, expanding you to life?

There are a number of mental pathways or stories we can tell ourselves in the aftermath of a life-changing experience. We can ruminate, our thoughts going around in circles: *I can't stop thinking about what happened, I don't know who I am or what I believe in.* Secondly, we can create a negative story: *This has ruined my life. I believe I am worse off because this happened;* or thirdly, we can create a positive story: *I am a better person because of this experience, this has made me stronger/more loving/more patient/more kind. This has changed me, and my life, for the better.*

The third option – seeing challenging circumstances in a positive light – is not our default mode. Our default mode tends to be the first and second mental pathways: rumination and worst case scenario. The 'Third Path', according to Positive Psychologist Shawn Achor, is the mental path that seeks to *make sense* of our circumstances, where we seek to construct a belief that, in fact, we are stronger and more capable than we were before our adversity.

Making sense or meaning of our challenges through a narrative of growth is empowering, resulting in a more positive outlook on life itself – but you're going to have to fight against your natural tendencies.

Through self-awareness, mindfulness and patience, we can find the mental pathway that gives us a choice about how we make sense of the difficulties we find ourselves in. We *can* choose the narrative, or the story we tell ourselves, in response to adversity. This takes time. It takes time to learn how to respond, not react, to the cacophony of fearful thoughts and negative emotions. And this is what you are on this journey to learn. Ask yourself:

What is the narrative, or story, that you have created from the situation that happened to you? Do you blame this thing for the state of your life right now? Do you believe that you are more capable? Are you proud of yourself for getting through the challenge and believe you can face adversity in the future again? Or do you believe that you are broken from this experience and that nothing good can come of it?

If we want to grow and transform from challenging life circumstances, we must take the time to examine and let go of beliefs that are no longer working for us and replace them with ones that are more positive and useful.

Check in with yourself: *What belief do you hold about your capacity to grow through challenge? What do you want to believe about yourself, with regards to this experience?*

I won't be surprised if your mind is saying: 'I can't change.' But if you can hear that resistance, something powerful is taking place. You are noticing your thoughts – that in itself is the core of self-awareness. You're about to shine a light on these monsters, so they have nowhere to hide.

The torch

Check yourself: do you ever find yourself going over conversations repeatedly, getting caught up in the details and unable to zoom out? Do you have moments where your stress or emotions overrun you, and you don't even realise how you're feeling until hours later? Do you find yourself saying things you don't mean, snapping, being defensive or passive-aggressive? Do you find yourself looking down only to realise you've finished the whole bag of Doritos without even noticing?

If the monsters in your head get the better of you, you're not alone. Research from psychologists Killingsworth and Gilbert of Harvard University shows that people spend '46.9 percent of their waking hours thinking about something other than what they're doing, and this mind-wandering typically makes them unhappy'. Being lost in our thoughts appears to be our brain's default mode of operating: recalling the past (deliberating about what we 'could have' or 'should have' done differently), thinking about the future (planning and being concerned with what we 'need to do'), or contemplating things that might not even happen.

Being caught up with these thoughts affects our stress levels and can lead to symptoms of anxiety or depression when they spiral out of control. (Be honest: how many times have you drifted off while reading this? How many of those thoughts were related to something you're worried about?)

The solution lies in not controlling our thoughts, but learning to 'be with them': 'Many philosophical and religious traditions teach that happiness is to be found by living in the moment, and practitioners are trained to resist mind wandering and to "be here now",' Killingsworth and Gilbert assert. What would it mean for you to create space from the monsters in your head, to see your thoughts as just thoughts, and not truth? How would your life be different if you could recognise your emotions and moods quicker? How would it help you to slow down and get perspective on your behaviours and reactions?

***

When you were a child, perhaps you were afraid of monsters under the bed. Your parents very likely would have had to shine a torch into the shadows below just to show you that the monsters weren't real. When it comes to the monsters in our heads, we need another type of torch: self-awareness.

Self-awareness is the light that can stop the monsters in their tracks, allowing you to observe them objectively and with some distance. It can help you to recognise that the monsters aren't *you*, but a *part of you.*

When we develop our torch of self-awareness, it gives us options on how to react when things are tough. Self-awareness is a superpower. It's your lightsabre that cuts through your preconceived notions of a situation, diminishing the strength of self-criticism and judgement. It is a tool that allows you to pause, reflect and act. With self-awareness comes *perspective.*

It's time for you to develop this torch of self-awareness with your monsters and consider how they affect your feelings and behaviours.

Exercise 1: Meeting Your Monsters

The purpose of this exercise is for you to practise turning on the torch of self-awareness by identifying the monsters in your head and their relationship to your feelings and behaviours. This exercise will also help you recognise if there are any thinking, emotional or behavioural patterns evident that you have been unaware of.

You will need a notepad and pen for this exercise. If you aren't currently listening to the playlist designed to accompany this book, perhaps you'd like to press play on it now, so you can listen while you work through the rest of this chapter. It will also help you reflect while you work through the exercise. Instructions to find the playlist *Darkness is Golden: Music for Reading* can be found at the beginning of this book.

Draw up three columns in your notepad. These will be labelled 'Thoughts', 'Feelings' and 'Behaviours' (see below for an example).

What are the monsters in your head telling you about your life and yourself as a person? To begin this exercise, think about a time in your life when you tried to do something and didn't get the result you hoped for. It could be a test or audition, or even assembling furniture. What was the narrative you told yourself when this happened? What did you replay in your head about your life? Write down your answers in the column labelled 'Thoughts' – they are your monsters.

How do these monsters in your head make you feel? They might be uncomfortable or unpleasant feelings, such as shame or disappointment. Write these down in the column labelled 'Feelings'.

What do these thoughts and feelings make you do or not do? For example, do you withdraw from social activities, emotionally eat, or overwork? Think about how you act when you are faced with a difficult situation. Write down your reactions in the column 'Behaviours'.

Examples:
THE MONSTERS IN YOUR HEAD

THOUGHTS	FEELINGS	BEHAVIOURS
I'm not enough	Sadness	Emotional eating
I'm not doing enough	Anger	Working harder
I'm useless	Shame	Drinking alcohol
People are judging me	Regret	Scrolling on phone
I'm not good enough	Guilt	Not exercising
I can't trust people	Disappointment	Withdrawing
There's no point to life	Loneliness	Watching shows
I don't know what to do	Anxiety	Cleaning your house
I can't overcome this	Numbness	Worrying
I'm not smart enough	Despair	Faking happiness
I'm ugly	Depression	People-pleasing
I hate myself	Insecurity	Being defensive
My life is terrible	Disgust	Obsessing
No-one is there for me	Disconnectedness	Staying in bed

Strengthening your torch through mindfulness

Your torch of self-awareness can be strengthened and we're going to work through some of the exercises that will help, like regular journalling, seeking therapy or a trusted friend's opinion, and mindfulness.

Mindfulness is the ability to pay attention on purpose. One way that it is practised is through paying attention to your senses – it can quite literally help you stop to smell the roses. When applied to your thoughts, it helps you develop space from them, allowing you to be aware of them, and giving you a choice in how to respond to them.

Practising mindfulness can help you take a few giant steps back – to notice *how* you are thinking. You can stand back and realise, 'Hey, I'm actually in a shitty mood right now. Is that framing my thoughts?' You are granted the option to recognise your frame of mind and redirect your attention to your present-moment experience.

You can also practise mindfulness by listening to meditations. Even if you have tried meditations before and found it difficult to pay attention, the ones I have designed for you have been created to calm and soothe the monsters and keep your mind focused. My own research has shown that carefully considered music paired with vocal guidance can have a huge effect on your ability to relax and concentrate.

I recommend practising at least one of these meditations daily to help you strengthen your torch of self-awareness. Think of it as an essential tool – by doing this you are exercising your mind, and strengthening your stability and grounding as we continue to navigate your darkness. Remember, you can come back to these meditations at any time on your journey.

We don't have to live our lives in our heads, consumed by our monsters of anxiety and worry. It's exhausting. You have a choice in how they impact your life.

AUDIO EXPERIENCES: MEDITATIONS

These meditations are designed to help you strengthen your self-awareness through a variety of grounding techniques and can be practised at any time of the day, either sitting up in a chair or lying down (if you're not prone to falling asleep!).

For the optimal experience, use headphones and listen to these in a quiet place where you won't be disturbed.

All of the audio experiences can be accessed by the QR code or website at the front of the book. 🎧

Audio Experience 1: ***When I Listen, I Open*** **(8 minutes)**

This is a simple meditation to help you to ground through listening deliberately to the sounds and tones of the music. Sound is a great anchor point for when you feel like the monsters in your head are getting out of control.

Audio Experience 2: ***Back to the Breath*** **(10 minutes)**

This meditation practice will help you develop your focus and concentration so you can be more aware of the monsters in your head, and learn to accept them without judging them. You might find that your mind wants to wander, but this doesn't mean you're doing it 'wrong'. By centring this practice on breath, you can create an anchor point to return to when you get distracted.

Audio Experience 3: *A Slow Release* (10 minutes)

When you have problems sleeping, this meditation will draw attention to different parts of your body, guiding you to tense and loosen each area to aid relaxation. When your body is in a more relaxed state, you will find that your mind will also be less busy.

Exercise 2: Journalling for Self-reflection

These journal prompts are your new daily practice of self-reflection, designed to strengthen your torch of self-awareness and help you to confront the monsters in your head. By writing down what you noticed during the day (thoughts, feelings, behaviours) in a journal, this will help you start to recognise your thought patterns and habits. It doesn't mean that they will stop automatically, but this is a good first step.

The best way to create a habit of journalling is to decide on a time of day, such as first thing in the morning, or before bed, and stick to it. If you are journalling in the morning, you will be reviewing the previous day. Give yourself at least fifteen minutes for a journalling session; you'll likely find yourself writing longer!

If you experience a particularly difficult day, you could try to find fifteen minutes to go through these questions; for example, during your lunch break at work.

Journalling prompts:
- What did you notice about your thoughts today?
- What did you notice about your feelings today? What were they?
- What did you notice about your behaviours today? What were they?
- Did you notice any patterns or habits in your thoughts, feelings or behaviours?

Skeletons: the root cause of your patterns

Have you ever found that there are some habits or patterns that are really hard to break, no matter how much self-awareness you shine on them? Having an awareness of your monsters and their impact on your feelings and behaviours is just the first step to understanding how these patterns are created. To transform them, however, we need to dig a little deeper to understand where they came from in the first place.

Standing in the dark lobby of the haunted house, you shine your torch over the corner of the room. On the ground, you'll see the handle of a trap door that will lead you into the secret basement of the house. Here, you'll enter the space that holds the skeletons of your past: the challenging experiences that have caused you pain and disappointment. These same skeletons filter into your conscious thoughts and feelings. They are the root cause of your patterns.

You might think that you're calling the shots, that you know why you think and act the way you do, but your actions are often driven by the *subconscious* rather than the *conscious* mind – exerting tremendous influence over you. It absorbs or rejects information based on your perceptions, which are based on past experiences, starting from the time you were born. Experiences in your childhood, adolescence and adulthood all contribute to these perceptions – the lens through which you see the world. For example, your dynamics with your parents growing up have a huge influence on how you relate to others in your adult relationships.

You might have experienced the impact of your skeletons: old insecurities resurfacing in your new relationship just when you thought you had your shit together; a part of you that still feels insecure despite your 'success'; your past 'failures' snaking their way into your self-decision-making.

When my clients start to dig up their skeletons, they are often surprised with what they find, and how it impacts their life. For example, one client, a corporate lawyer, Kim, came to therapy to work on her pattern of being overly critical of new partners. Her relationships would start well but end quickly as she found herself picking apart her suitors before they could get close. Without realising, she was pushing them away. Delving into her skeletons, we found that she had been deeply hurt by a break-up in university and was still carrying the pain of that relationship subconsciously. The break-up had come out of nowhere and caused her to doubt her sense of judgement in choosing partners for herself. At the heart of it, her subconscious fear of getting hurt again caused her to keep potential partners at arm's length and judge them prematurely. In acknowledging her past hurt, she was able to recognise when her fear kicked in with someone new, and slowly open up to new relationships without her typical knee-jerk reactions.

Exercise 3: Meet Your Skeletons

This exercise is designed to help you uncover the root causes of your habit patterns. While reading over your responses from Exercise 1: Meeting Your Monsters, your task is to identify the situations in your childhood, adolescence, adulthood or recent past that may be at the root of your challenging thoughts, feelings and behaviour patterns. Some examples of past experiences could be a relationship or friendship break-up, the death of someone you love, being bullied in school, failing something important, or being socially rejected or excluded. Nothing is insignificant in this space: no matter how small they may seem, write those moments down in your journal.

Go gently here: there may be experiences that are tough for you to remember.

You might be tempted to skip this exercise because it makes you feel uncomfortable, but don't – this is a really important one on your transformational path.

You are not alone

Over the course of writing this book I also had a frightening number of monsters and skeletons to confront.

I had a pattern of burning out – working so hard, getting overwhelmed, taking a short break ... but returning to the same habits of overextending myself. My monsters would always push me to do more, and be there for others more than myself. Opening up my digital calendar would give me instant anxiety – every minute was full. Eight clients a day? No issues; load 'em up. Meetings squished into my lunch break; workshops every night and weekend; go, go, go. There was no space in my calendar to take care of myself; I was living an unsustainable life with little emotional energy for myself.

Changing my behaviour didn't help. In the midst of my business's madness I dreamt of what life would be like if I could be creative every day. Surely, that would fix all my problems. But then, when I started committing myself to this book, I just replaced those anxiety attacks over the business with anxiety attacks over a chapter. On the surface, my life had changed. But deep down, I was operating from that very same place, just as insecure as ever. It was happening again.

To get to the core of my habits, I had to face the thoughts that would tell me that opening my emails after dinner was a good idea; the ones that would egg me on to get up to create new ideas for the business while falling asleep in bed. I had to notice their impact: I felt burdened by the weight of responsibility; I'd wake up feeling like a truck hit me. I sometimes couldn't get out of bed the day after an event. My core belief: I'm not good enough (unless I'm doing something for others or kicking goals).

I had to face my skeletons: childhood experiences where my accomplishments at school meant I got attention. Getting twenty dollars for every A on my report card. Not getting into a medical degree and feeling the disappointment of my parents. Being cheated on. Being betrayed by friends.

Healing my negative self-beliefs was going to take more than telling myself that I was loveable or taking a week off work. I had to develop the light of my torch of self-awareness and confront the creatures in my house. I had to be my own 'ghostbuster', slaying monsters not with a vacuum but with a light from within.

If the process of turning on your torch illuminates just how much of a mess your haunted house is in ... I get it. It can be a shock to confront feelings that you've been ignoring or to spot the beliefs that are holding you back. It can also feel like a huge pain, but it's actually an enormous achievement, taking this first step to becoming more aware of your thoughts, self-beliefs and the past experiences that shaped them. You can't work with something you can't see.

If you're finding these exercises overwhelming, I'd encourage you to give yourself space and time to sit with the feelings that arise by practising the meditations. The first couple of weeks of a journey like this can often be the hardest.

The path of personal transformation is like walking into a dark room where things slowly become clearer as your eyes adjust. At first, everything is frightening and uncertain, until you begin to see in the dark, exploring nooks and crevices, corners and hidden objects. This is the growth of self-awareness. You discovering you.

You are no longer the child who is afraid of the dark. You are an adult who is remembering that fear but starting to understand how it affects you today. You are acknowledging your feelings and behaviours. The torch of self-awareness is coming on, and it will get brighter as you learn how to wield it. Your mind once filled in the gaps of the unknown with the scariest creatures imaginable. But you are now slowly breaking that illusion and the glimpses of reality are beginning to show.

This takes courage, and you are brave. Remember to go slow, so your eyes can adjust to what's really there, not just what you think is there. Take your time in these rooms. Revel in the dust underneath the sofa, the junk in the drawers you never open, and all the stuff that's fallen through the cracks over the years. Paint the walls gold with your awareness.

The next room awaits.

CHAPTER 3

'I Just Want to Be Happy'

In Defence of Emotions (All of Them)

A journey through the darkness, hand in hand with our skeletons is no mean feat. The first step is tough: digging them up and acknowledging they exist. But after that we must sit with them, brush off the soil caked onto their bones and breathe life into them, letting their cracked jaws tell us their stories. Really, they are your stories – the fragments of your life that have made you *you*.

Hearing these stories can be painful. They tell of traumas, losses and disappointments. They hold the pain of memories trapped in the remains of their body. When you hold their bones, you feel sadness, regret, frustration and anger. These are the feelings that you have buried and run away from.

Your skeletons – these painful past experiences – are the root cause of your patterns. This is where it all begins. When you first turn on the torch of self-awareness, illuminating the dark corners of your mind, it can be hard to confront what you find in the shadows. But this is an exploration that is worth it.

Unearthing your skeletons of past pain can be so overwhelming that you hurry to bury them again. Why? Because of how these memories make you *feel*. If you could look back on past pain and feel it was genuinely resolved; if you could think of something that made you anxious but not be overwhelmed by it; if you could be more rational about your fears, it wouldn't be such a battle. These skeletons bring up challenging feelings and it's only natural that we'd want to run away from them.

How can we face the darkness within our uncomfortable emotions? How can we learn to recognise those emotions when they arise, and acknowledge them without getting overwhelmed? How can we learn to accept our emotions, rather than running from them? How can we work with our emotions to find self-acceptance?

Why do we avoid our emotions?

If you don't completely understand emotions, no-one can really blame you. A true understanding of how emotions work sits at the intersection of evolutionary, physiological, psychological, cultural and societal studies – and I don't expect you to have five university degrees.

Our societal and cultural values encourage us to try to be happy all the time. Yet the way society expects us to do so is often in direct conflict with the objective itself. Our culture is obsessed with the pursuit of 'external achievement' and outward appearances; it tells us that if we earn more money, are more attractive and have more things, we'll be happier. But we won't. Despite many of us knowing that 'money doesn't buy happiness', we still fall into the trap of overestimating how happy the next materialistic milestone will make us. We neglect the importance of our emotional wellbeing as we focus on scouring the horizons for our next 'achievement'.

We pursue happiness voraciously, yet research shows that chasing happiness only makes us unhappier. *Toxic positivity,* the denial or repression of our authentic emotions in favour of being 'happy' or 'positive', is rife in the world today. Social media bombards us with bite-sized pep talks: 'be positive', 'be grateful', and 'live your best life'. But it neglects to show us how to do any of this, leaving many of us feeling like we are failing when we don't feel happy all the goddamn time.

If 'feeling good' means not feeling any 'negative' emotions, a pursuit of fulfilment is destined for disappointment.

***

From a physiological perspective, feeling distressing emotions is uncomfortable. Whether we are conscious of it or not, emotions cause sensations throughout our body, causing us physical discomfort that we consciously or subconsciously want to suppress or move away from.

Emotional pain registers in the same area of the brain as physical pain, the *anterior cingulate cortex* – this is why we say it 'hurts' when we feel rejected or unloved. We feel heartbreak, rejection and losses viscerally: anxiety feels like cats cartwheeling in our stomach, grief like we're moving through jelly, depression like we're drowning underwater. It makes sense that we'd want to avoid all of this.

You avoid uncomfortable emotions not just because of the pain they inflict but also as a result of *learned behaviours,* things you've picked up from family, friends and workplaces, and integrated into your value system as your own.

Growing up, I instinctively avoided certain emotions. My family never really spoke about how they felt or expressed emotions openly. I can't recall anyone asking me, *How are you really?,* with the intention of getting to the heart of how I was feeling.

In my family of Vietnamese refugees, emotions were seen as a weakness, something that got in the way of 'showing face' – we were taught to put our best foot forward in order to portray an image of success to other families. As is often the case with Asian families, the focus was on external achievement: getting good grades, becoming a doctor or lawyer and making money. We were not encouraged to think about emotional health or open up about our feelings.

Perhaps you grew up in a similar household. You might look back and realise that particular emotions were judged or suppressed. You may have learnt that being sad or angry were 'bad' emotions, which meant if you ever expressed these feelings you were punished, but rewarded if you were cheerful, happy or quiet. Perhaps you changed your own behaviour to accommodate someone else's emotions, hiding your own feelings or walking on eggshells in fear of someone else being upset or angry.

In therapy, it is very important for me to understand how a client's emotions were expressed and received throughout their childhood. It is also important for me to understand how their parents or primary caregivers managed or expressed their emotions. Clients often tell me that their parents (although loving) didn't know how to talk about how they were feeling, were uncomfortable with expressing vulnerabilities, and that they showed love through other ways, rather than expressing it verbally.

They all have very good reasons for understanding why their parents had a lack of emotional openness and vulnerability ('that was just how they showed love', 'they were focused on creating a stable family life', 'but I knew that they cared about me') but often downplay the impact a lack of emotional connectedness had on them in later life. What we've been taught (or not taught) about emotions filters into the way we deal with our own feelings and how we act when we hit rough patches in life.

Have you ever found yourself holding back your feelings with your friends in fear of being a 'burden' or 'downer'? Do you wear a mask that portrays the sense that 'it's all good', smiling even through a down or anxious day? Have you ever berated yourself to 'get over it' when you're in a bad mood, or been annoyed at yourself for feeling depressed or anxious? If you have, you aren't alone. I have done all of these things. Even after years of working on this, I still sometimes 'catch' my inner voice giving me a hard time for not feeling 'great'. We must recognise that our tendencies to disregard our own feelings are shaped by our lived experience – from childhood to this very moment.

Emotional regulation

Now that we recognise that our emotions are here to stay, how are we going to deal with them?

Emotional regulation is the term used to describe the different ways we influence our emotions. We each employ different strategies to do this, often without being aware of their impacts.

In a study by Stanford University, emotions expert Professor James Gross looked at the difference between two strategies for regulating emotions – *suppression* and *reappraisal* – and their implication for how we experience emotions, wellbeing and social relationships.

Reappraisal of emotions involves *changing the way we think* about situations we are in. In contrast, emotional repression involves *not expressing* – inhibiting or concealing emotion. In Gross's study, participants were asked to watch a 'disgusting film' and split into three groups. The first group was told to think about the film so they would not respond emotionally (reappraisal group), the second to hide their emotions so that a person watching them would not know that they were feeling anything (suppression), and the third to simply just watch the film (control). Participants were videotaped, their physiological responses monitored, and they were also asked about their subjective experience.

The participants who suppressed their emotions *expressed* fewer negative emotions, but still reported *experiencing* as many negative emotions as people who weren't told to suppress them. Suppression participants also experienced greater *sympathetic activation* of their nervous system than participants who just watched the film – basically, the body was showing signs that suppressing their emotions was actually causing them more stress.

So, what happens if we chronically suppress our emotions? In another study, Gross measured people with an Emotion Regulation Questionnaire (ERQ) and found that people who routinely pushed their feelings away experienced even *more* of the negative emotions that they were trying to avoid and fewer positive emotions. Ignoring our uncomfortable emotions actually causes us more pain in the long term. It's akin to spraining your ankle and trying to ignore it, only to find you've damaged the muscle by continuing to walk on it.

Suppressing emotions comes at a cost. Not only does it inhibit your positive emotions, but it's linked to being more depressed, having a decreased satisfaction with life, lower self-esteem and decreased optimism. Studies also suggest that the 'tight control of negative emotions may adversely affect physical health', and increase stress. Researchers have proposed that this may be because people have the sense that 'they are not being authentic or true to themselves when they suppress emotions'.

The negative effect of emotional suppression also filters into relationships. In a study of couples, Emily Impett and her colleagues found that when one partner suppresses their emotions, *both* partners have lower emotional wellbeing and are less satisfied in their relationships. Impett also found that those who suppressed their emotions were also *more* likely to think about breaking up with their partners three months later. We've all experienced the unintended consequences of suppression – snapping at loved ones, unexpectedly finding ourselves crying in the office toilets or getting triggered over a mild situation like someone not taking the garbage out.

We bypass and suppress our uncomfortable emotions in so many ways: have you ever found yourself standing in front of the fridge even though you've just had lunch? Poured yourself a glass of wine after work without even thinking? Even habits like overanalysing or worrying can be ways in which we bypass feeling uncomfortable emotions.

But not all avoidances are so obvious. Most insidious are the ways we avoid feeling uncomfortable emotions through actions that are socially acceptable – routinely staying back late in the office, manic exercise, diverting all our energy into 'helping others'. Our avoidance mechanisms are sneaky. The behaviours that people praise us for the most can be the ones we have to keep an eye on – they may be masking our fear of sitting with discomfort.

Emotions are here to help us

Emotions aren't the bad guys – without them, life would be oh-so-dull. Imagine eating an ice-cream and feeling ... nothing. Sex ... nothing. But even outside of feeling pleasure and happiness, emotions that we typically avoid, like anger, can be useful too. What would drive us to change the world without some fire in our bellies? What would drive us to connect with each other if we never felt lonely? Even guilt has its place: it allows us to reflect upon our behaviour when we've hurt others.

The experience of emotional pain has an evolutionary advantage. Like physical pain, thirst and hunger, emotional pain is an aversive state that pushes us to change our behaviour in order to increase our capacity for survival. Over hundreds and thousands of years, we have learnt that together we are stronger. The emotional pain of loneliness then, for example, is rooted deeply in the human need for connection, a signal for us to reach out to others and create loving connections to ensure our survival.

We need to drop the idea that there are 'good' or 'bad' emotions and recognise that feeling them all, helps us. According to psychologist Paul Ekman, a pioneer in emotion research, 'Emotions wouldn't have been preserved over the course of evolution if they were intrinsically harmful or destructive in any way.' They are part of a complex appraisal system that can help us to make decisions and keep us safe from harm. 'Our fear emotions can save our lives,' explains Ekman. 'It's what we use to help us turn out of the way of a vehicle that's headed towards us without thinking. If we had to think about this situation and get ourselves out of trouble, we'd be dead.'

Emodiversity

What if you allowed yourself to open up and play the full range of emotional chords? Otherwise known as *emodiversity,* feeling a variety of emotions has been shown to predict mental and physical health. In two studies with over 37,000 participants, Jordi Quoidbach (Pompeu Fabra University, Barcelona) and his team of researchers demonstrated that those who report experiencing a wide variety of emotions have better markers for mental and physical health, such as decreased depression and doctor visits.

These findings build upon research that reveals how people who have a 'rich, authentic, and complex emotional life' are more self-aware, live more authentic lives and have greater wellbeing and resilience. Feeling all the feels, whether they come as sunny days, dark stormy nights or everything in between, is the key to the experience of contentment.

Think about the people you admire in your life, the ones you would seek guidance from if you were in a rut. Are they not the same people who aren't afraid to express their emotions and speak openly about their challenges? Are they people who've been through the trenches, who aren't afraid to acknowledge the messiness of life? These are typically the folk that inspire us most. When we see someone own their mistakes, and use them to transform their life, we want to connect with them. These qualities exist within you too.

We've often relegated personal growth and distress to opposite sides of a continuum. We have it in our heads that growing has to feel *good,* or that feeling uncomfortable is a sign that we are failing to grow. Flip that idea on its head: *you can grow while feeling pain.* In fact, emotional pain can be a key sign that you are growing and ready for change.

Opening yourself to the experience of emotional pain, little by little, is akin to the growth we see in our muscles: they break down during exercise, only to rebuild stronger. The process of personal transformation is much the same: 'breaking down' a little to rebuild a house that can withstand the winds of life.

Emotions as a pathway to self-acceptance

You have now met some of your monsters (thoughts that challenge you), and your skeletons (painful past experiences). The next step into the dark is learning to identify, accept and feel the emotions that are coming up as a result of these thoughts and past experiences.

We're going to name the uncomfortable emotions that arise from the monsters in your mind and the skeletons from your past. We'll call them your *spirits,* and examples of these are emotions like anger, annoyance, fear, anxiety, sadness, guilt and apathy.

You feel more emotions than you realise. You might like to refer to the Wheel of Emotions to appreciate them all.

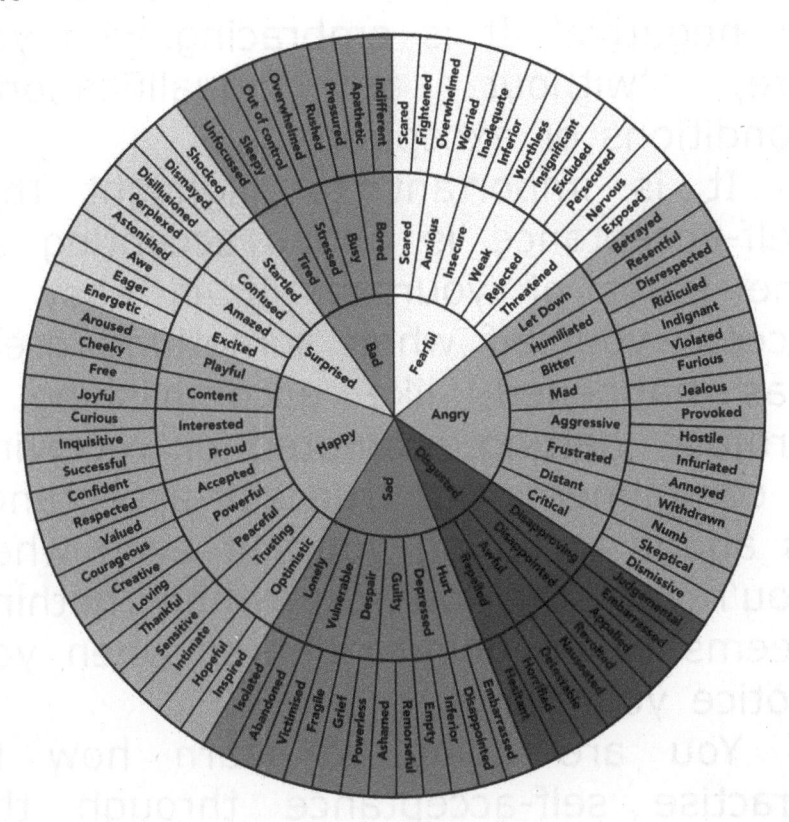

You've learnt some of the ways emotions can be helpful. But more than anything else, entering the darkness and developing a relationship with your spirits brings forth the gold of *self-acceptance*.

According to research from Fabiane Morgardo and her colleagues from the University of Campinas, Brazil, self-acceptance is 'an individual's acceptance of their attributes, positive or negative'. It is embracing who you are, 'without any qualifications, conditions or exceptions'.

It is important to highlight that self-acceptance is about accepting *all* the parts of yourself. It is easy to accept yourself when something great has happened, like accomplishing a project, getting promoted or receiving a compliment. But true self-acceptance is about accepting yourself even when you're in the dumps, when nothing seems to be going right or when you notice your flaws.

You are going to learn how to practise self-acceptance through the feeling and acceptance of your *emotions* – the spirits that whirl up in reaction to everything you think and do. Think of it this way: when we reject our uncomfortable emotions, we are essentially rejecting ourselves. We are telling ourselves that our normal reactions to pain are 'not okay'. If you do this repeatedly, you are continually turning your back on yourself. We are here to rekindle that neglected relationship.

I like to encourage my clients to check in with themselves in the morning, as soon as they wake up – somewhere in between their eyes opening and the moment they reach for their phone. And I ask you to do this too. In those hazy first seconds of the day, ask yourself, 'How are you?' Sometimes the answer may be 'Flat. Unmotivated. Anxious'. When this is our response, we typically default to reacting – by doing everything we can to change that state. But what I'd like you to consider is that listening to those feelings – whatever they may be – and gently accepting them is actually a way of accepting *yourself*. Try saying to yourself: 'It's okay for you to feel this way' in these moments. It's a simple gesture that can change your life over time.

Accepting your emotions, no matter how messy they get, is a testament to your *relationship with yourself.* When you acknowledge and accept your emotions by feeling them, you are telling yourself that *you matter.* That what you experienced was hard and your feelings are valid. This is akin to being your own best friend.

Treat yourself how you would treat someone you really care about when they are going through a tough time, by being supportive, accepting and non-judgemental. This involves letting yourself feel whatever is coming up for you – letting yourself cry, feel anxious or angry. I like to visualise self-acceptance as building a bridge back to yourself, a form of reconnection and healing from judgement and self-criticism.

To start to develop a relationship with your spirits, first you need to identify them. Feeling into them will then create a pathway to self-acceptance.

Spirits in the body

We now need to tune you into the sensations in your body to strengthen your ability to recognise your spirits (uncomfortable emotions). Happiness, for example, is typically characterised by sensations of lightness and space in the body, whereas anger or sadness can be felt as tension, heaviness and tightness in areas of the body, typically around the throat, stomach or chest.

Body-centred practices such as dance, yoga and meditation can help you become more attuned to your bodily sensations, which helps you regulate your emotions. Not all meditations are created equal – body-based meditations such as body scanning are the most useful for improving emotion regulation. They focus on strengthening your ability to feel emotions and sensations without judgement. This ability is a skill that helps you to reduce reactions such as avoidance, distraction, numbing or projection of your emotions onto others.

Whenever I work with clients, we always start with the body. We can get so caught up trying to work everything out in our heads, it's easy to feel confused about what we're actually feeling – but the body never lies. So,

I'm going to take you through a few exercises designed to help you identify, feel and express your emotions, with a focus on where they arise in your body. Learning to feel your emotions can be challenging if you are new to this, so go slow if you need to, and remember that you can always return to your meditations in Chapter 2 to help you ground yourself. Personally, when I feel resistant towards these exercises I remind myself of something my good friend Ali once said to me: 'You gotta feel to heal.' You got this.

Exercise 1: Meet Your Spirits

Step 1: Identify your emotions
Your first step is to learn how to identify your emotions. You can practise this by asking yourself how you feel.

What emotions are you feeling as a result of digging up the skeletons of your past hurts and monsters in your mind? Examples could be: loneliness, anger, anxiety, guilt, shame, resentment, fear, sadness, longing, disappointment, fear and numbness.

To help you get in touch with these emotions, gently recall some of the past experiences that you identified in the last chapter (Chapter 2, Exercise 4: Meet Your Skeletons). Take some time to write down your feelings in your journal. They may be singular words, or you might like to go into more detail. Try not to overthink it – sit with your impulse responses. When you feel you've captured them, move on to Step 2.

Step 2: Noticing the emotions in your body

This part of the exercise will guide you through what your emotions feel like in your body when they arise. It will help you to identify how you hold tension in the body as a response to stress and challenges, and provide you with some techniques that will allow you to observe the sensations in your body more objectively.

Understanding the areas of your body that reflect your stress-response will help you to 'sit in', accept and feel your feelings when a stressful situation arises in the future.

I'm going to give you two options for exploring this exercise. One you can listen to on your phone: a sonic embodiment called *The Darkness Immersion.* The other can be read and followed below, under the title *Noticing the Spirits.*

Audio Experience 4: The Darkness Immersion

A sonic embodiment is an immersive audio experience that fuses music and meditation-like guidance to 'embody' you – that is, allow you to experience specific emotions, and be cradled through those feelings.

The Darkness Immersion is a 13-minute audio experience designed to help you observe and sit with difficult emotions. You will need headphones and a quiet place where you won't be disturbed.

To access this audio experience, turn to the front of the book to access the QR code or browser address, or open your saved Spotify playlist: *Darkness is Golden: Audio Experiences.* 🎧

Noticing the Spirits in Your Body (self-guided)

While the audio experience is recommended, this self-guided exercise will also help you observe and sit with difficult emotions.

Take a few deep breaths and focus in on your body. Think back to one of your skeletons – a situation from your past that caused you pain. Notice how it feels in the body as you remember that situation. Take your attention to a part of your body that feels the most uncomfortable, perhaps around the throat, chest or stomach.

Focus on the sensations in this area for a minute, observing what you feel.

To observe the sensations objectively, use these questions as a guide:

1. Do these sensations feel light or heavy?
2. Do these sensations have a shape or colour?

3. Are these sensations still or moving?

4. Do these sensations have a temperature? For example, are they warm, cool, hot?

5. Can you describe the emotions that you are experiencing? For example, can you feel sadness, frustration, anxiety?

Using this diagram (you can also copy it into your journal), colour in the parts of your body where you noticed sensations such as tension, heaviness or tightness.

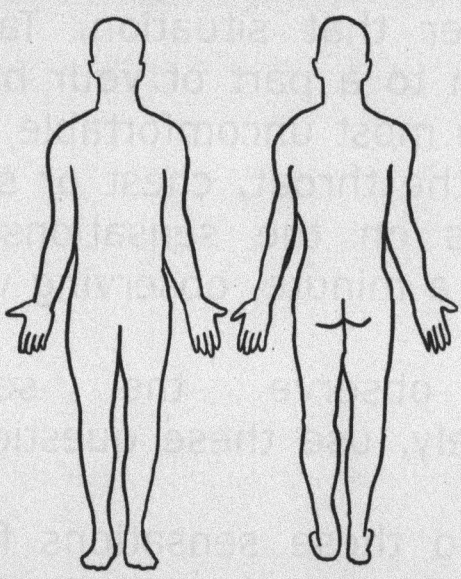

When you have completed the sonic embodiment or self-guided

exercise, complete the process by using these journal prompts to help you to understand and reflect on your experience:
- What sensations did you feel?
- Did you notice that you wanted to move away from or get rid of the sensations?
- What was it like to 'sit in your feelings'?
- If you listened to the audio exercise, how did the music affect your experience?
- If you completed the drawing activity, where did you feel the sensations of your emotions the most? What would help you notice these emotions in your body more during the day?

Audio Experience 5: Awaken the Body (15 minutes)

The purpose of this meditation is to develop a connection with the sensations in your body, and therefore with your emotions and yourself. This audio experience will help you to notice sensations without trying to push them away, and learn to accept what you're feeling. Add this 12-minute practice to your daily meditations to help you to develop more awareness of sensations in your body.

Paying attention to our spirits doesn't mean that you will be consumed by them. Feeling them, rather than thinking about them, allows them to be visitors that come and go. This is the nature of *impermanence:* that all things change. Experiencing your emotions as impermanent through this meditation will give you the ability to practise 'letting them be' when they arise throughout your day.

To access this audio experience, turn to the front of the book to access the QR code or browser address, or else open your saved Spotify playlist: *Darkness is Golden: Audio Experiences.* 🎧

Expressing your spirits through writing

Writing can be extremely beneficial in helping you acknowledge and feel your emotions. The following exercise is one my therapist shared with me, and one that I continue to use with myself and my clients. Writing a letter (that you don't send) to someone in your past or present who hurt you, or with whom you have unresolved issues, allows you to honour, express and process any feelings you may have repressed. We don't always have the chance to say how we really feel, so this exercise provides a vital outlet.

Some relationships are so destructive, it would be dangerous for you to express yourself openly. Perhaps they are with people who are unable to really 'hear' you. Alternatively, some of these relationships might be with people who you'll never cross paths with again. Writing a letter to them without sending it means that you can be completely honest and not censor yourself out of fear of being judged or rejected.

This exercise will take roughly one hour to complete, and it would be best if you can find a quiet space to write in. There may be more than one person you want to write to, but I would suggest you write just one letter this first time and leave the rest for another day, to give you space to sit with the emotions that come up.

Exercise 3: Letter Writing (The Purge)

Go back to your skeletons from Chapter 2 and choose a person connected to one of your painful experiences: they will be the addressee of your first letter. In this letter, begin by describing a situation you have experienced with them and how you really feel about what happened. Write down what you didn't get from the relationship, and how you have seen it affect your life. Don't censor yourself or try to make it 'nice'.

Be honest with yourself about how you feel and if you get angry, sad, or feel anything else, that's entirely okay.

If tears come, let them. Feel the words that you are writing. Remember, this is a letter that you won't send. This is a tool for you, intended to help you acknowledge, honour and purge your true feelings.

After you are done, I recommend taking some time out for yourself. Be mindful of how you are feeling in the days following this exercise. It's common to feel heavy, sensitive or tired for the next day or so. It might be helpful to write down the different feelings and thoughts that arise in you. If writing isn't something you connect with, you might prefer a different creative expression of these feelings, such as dance, art or music.

This exercise is an opportunity to be kind to yourself and practise self-care: rest, if you need it, or take a walk outside, meditate or find a place in nature where you can read or relax. It's all about learning to listen to your body and to respond to its needs.

If you aren't already listening to it, the playlist *Darkness is Golden:*

Music for Reading is a perfect accompaniment while you write your letters. You might also find listening to it is useful afterwards, when you're sitting with the emotions that bubble up through the exercise and reflecting upon your experience. If you're using the playlist this way, I recommend you find a quiet place where you won't be disturbed, use headphones, and lie down for comfort.

To access this audio experience, turn to the front of the book to access the QR code or browser address, or else open your saved Spotify playlist.

🎧

Grief and transformation

Now that you have discovered your spirits, it may help to understand that at the heart of the emotions you are experiencing is *grief*. Grief is what we call the collection of emotions we feel in response to the experience of loss. Feeling grief is a fundamental part of the process of personal transformation.

We often think of grief as the emotions felt in response to the loss of life, yet we grieve much more than just physical death. Think of your experiences in this way: if your life has changed, if you have had people leave you or the unexpected happen, you've experienced the death of a part of you: your identity, beliefs, attitudes or habits. Cast your mind back to the explanation for the conditions of post-traumatic growth (Chapter 1): when traumatic experiences occur, they create an earthquake that shatters the core beliefs of who you are. Personal growth is demonstrated by the way you reflect on those experiences and learn from them, rebuilding your core beliefs from the rubble. So, if you accept that at some point, one or more of your beliefs will be shattered, it makes sense to allow yourself to grieve the 'death' of those beliefs. In grieving them, you acknowledge who you were before the change, and the pain of your loss.

Grief is complex and not always connected to the obvious. Let's take the grief of a relationship breakdown as an example: you might feel the loss of that person in your life, but also the absence of shared plans for the future and hope for where you were heading. I remember sitting with a client of mine, Sam, who had just experienced a devastating break-up – he had been single for many years prior to the relationship and had placed a lot of hope in his new partner being 'the One', the break-up taking him by surprise.

A lot of his sadness was initially focused on missing 'her' and wishing things had worked out differently. It was important for me to help him see that his feelings of sadness and disappointment also stemmed from the grief of their shared dreams to start a family together, and even the little things like being able to share the details of his day via text, and having someone to say goodnight to before bed.

How did you grieve during the global pandemic? Did you have plans that were called off, your dreams on pause, your business crippled or a way of life change irrevocably? Millions of individuals and families have lost financial security and many have been plunged into social isolation and uncertainty. We are grieving 'old lives', our plans and ways of living, and we're having to adjust and accept the 'new normal'. The rollercoaster of emotions we're feeling collectively is grief.

Over the years, I've worked with athletes who are grieving the loss of their dreams, having had their careers end suddenly due to injury. Mothers and fathers grieving their loss of freedom and old identities in the shock of grappling with the drastic changes parenthood has wrought to their lifestyle. The loss may not always be obvious at the outset but is rooted in feelings of grief.

Grief can also come from experiences where we have felt invisible, unseen or unimportant in our lives. It can come from recognising that others were not there for us when we needed them – times when we have been ignored, rejected or neglected. Grief can also come from the pain of *not being there for ourselves.* This is the pain of being mean, unkind, critical and unforgiving towards ourselves.

Swiss-American psychiatrist and pioneer in near-death studies Elisabeth Kubler-Ross's 'stages of grief' outline some of the emotions and reactions that we have in response to loss: denial, anger, bargaining, depression and acceptance. If uncovering your skeletons has caused you to feel like you are in a washing machine of emotions, this is completely normal. You may have felt a kaleidoscope of emotions: anxiety, guilt, shame, acceptance and longing.

There is no 'right way' to grieve but feeling and accepting the kaleidoscope of emotions is the first step in processing this grief.

You are not alone

It was after writing this chapter that I had a breakdown.

Nothing had changed about my external world, but something within me fell apart as if it had. All the digging, reflection and combing through past memories brought up painful emotions – frequent and debilitating anxiety attacks, excruciating tightness in my chest and a pervasive sense of overwhelm and unease. I woke up with it, had my morning tea with it, ate with it, and got frustrated when it followed me to bed.

My therapist called it 'anxiety and mild depression', but at the heart of it, it was *pain:* the embodied experience of loneliness, sadness, insecurities, the grief of forgotten tears – and of forgetting myself. It was childhood pain as well as the way that it had bled into my adulthood. I didn't expect to fall apart while writing this book – you just can't plan these things. It was the last thing I wanted; it was probably everything I needed. Perhaps I was naïve to think that certain relationships and traumas in my life weren't going to rear their heads while poking them with a stick. Instead, I seemed destined to meet my monsters, skeletons and spirits in real time, with you.

The thought that I would be attempting to put myself back together so that I could then write about it, with deadlines looming, was not a comforting thought. I was a rat in my own experiment. *What if I fail? What if it takes me a year to feel better? What if I don't feel better?* It's very easy in a heightened state of anxiety to feel as though everything is impossible. I knew pain and grief had their own timepieces, and they sure didn't work on our schedules.

I stopped writing. Well, I tried to, but kept testing myself by opening my laptop to see how I would feel. My heart would start to race and try to beat out of my chest. My emails gave me palpitations. Everything got really hard. I felt very lost and vulnerable. I was like the student in the class who feels like everyone else is miles ahead. Definitely not the teacher.

The last chapter took over a year to complete. I initially went into microscopic detail about my first relationship and childhood pain and then edited them down when I'd get a rush of shame or embarrassment. I wanted to make it 'right' and 'perfect', mulling over and pulling apart these stories again and again.

I thought I had dampened my perfectionist tendencies. I had burnt myself out at work a few times, and the last time I made a pact to limit the things I was juggling. I wanted to enjoy the things I was creating. My grand plan was to step back from work to focus on writing – *immersing myself in creativity, a perfect plan to change the pace that I was working at!*

I'd made progress – unravelling myself from running a company was no easy task. But the dream of staring wistfully out the window while writing was met with the reality that I had never written a book before. What was my 'voice' and how did I find it? Wasn't it always meant to be there, and come pouring out of me? Why did the stuff I write one day seem genius then the next day horrific?

Old habits crept back into my life. Criticism. Judgement. Being mean to myself. Ignoring warning signs. Diminishing what I knew. Writing for ten to twelve hours a day. Scrapping most of it because it wasn't 'good enough'. What I was saying was that *I* wasn't good enough. But I persisted, as I always had, slimming down my already slim social schedule. Weekends! What weekends? The crippling self-doubt and insecurity fuelled my decision to 'work harder'.

I finished the chapter and I started having multiple-a-day anxiety and panic attacks. Dissociating. Having to lie down in yoga classes because my heart was racing and my head was dizzy. Feeling down, overwhelmed, extra sensitive. *Squeeze, squeeze, squeeze:* the pain of the heart as if someone was trying to rip it from its walls or compress it into a stone.

It felt like a cruel joke – was I really having a breakdown after writing about emotions? Have I been writing about feeling emotions while not feeling my emotions? The irony was overwhelmingly bitter.

I had to realise that it wasn't 'writing a book' that was necessarily bringing up feelings of anxiety, but an underlying belief that I wasn't good enough, which stemmed from something much deeper. I had to face the skeletons from my past that had led to these beliefs, learn to sit in the feelings of anxiety, and also delve into situations from my past where I had felt judged. Moments when I needed to 'be more' in order to be a valuable person. And I had to let myself feel all of those experiences.

In therapy, I felt like I was back at square one. I sat with my eyes closed a lot and felt the pain that was in my body. Recalling old memories that I wanted so much to put behind me. Dredging it all back up again. Trying to cry. Crying. Feeling numb. Getting frustrated. Feeling annoyed at myself. Feeling useless. Struggling with 'taking time out'. Writing letters. Seeing old patterns. Avoidance. Resistance. Moments of release. Then back to the pain.

Sometimes, we think our hearts have healed, but a lot of the time they only have flimsy bandaids on them, ones that start to curl up at the sides and make you itch at the sticky residue, at best a temporary solution. I thought time had healed some of my old memories but it became evident that I was still uncovering new layers to heal.

Breaking down to rebuild wasn't easy. But here's what changed things. I gave my uncomfortable feelings space, instead of resisting them. When I'd feel anxious, I'd stop what I was doing and pay attention to it, if only for a few minutes. Accepting the challenging feelings was a way to honour myself. A way of saying, 'No, this doesn't feel great. But this is me right now. And I accept it.'

Honouring our feelings is one of the most important yet challenging things we can do. We have to cradle them oh-so-gently, examine them with curiosity and compassion, and let them run rampant in our bodies, putting the weight of lead in our chests and bellies. It is only when we do so that the feelings tire themselves out. They get bored and move on.

We have to remember that our spirits aren't permanent residents in our haunted house – they come and they go. Although they may be unwelcome, and difficult to manage, they do leave us with a golden gift: learning to accept ourselves for how we show up in the moment. They point us towards our unmet grief and teach us the art of surrender. You are learning to have tenderness towards the parts of yourself that you want to reject – the parts that you may think have no purpose or beauty.

Remember, you can grow while feeling pain. You are working on the roots of the patterns that you experience in your life, and releasing emotions that have been held within you for a long time. Feel what you are ready to feel. Be gentle. Go slow.

At the end of the day, emotions come and go like the storms, the hail and the warm spring days. Our ability to stop, watch and surrender to it all is something that we must all learn: it is not something we have been conditioned to do. In the words of monk Pema Chödrön, 'You are the sky. Everything else – it's just the weather.'

CHAPTER 4

The Path Through Inner Conflict

Finding Wisdom When Nothing Makes Sense

With your torch shining on the grimy wooden floors, you travel to a room at the back of the house. As you enter, you are surprised. The space contains nothing but three large opulent mirrors with heavily carved gold frames, now chipped and faded with time. In front of them sits a couch of cracked mahogany leather. As you walk past each mirror, memories of yourself at different ages in your life flash before you. You are alone in all of them, and you can see clearly in your face that you are distressed, unhappy or angry at yourself. Sitting on the couch, you take in the scenes before you as if you were watching a movie of your life.

You are ready to meet the other parts of you that are reflected in the mirrors. They are glimpses of your *Inner Beings*: the *Inner Critic, Inner Saboteur* and *Inner Child.* With the torch of self-awareness shining on your *Inner Beings,* you will be able to see the voices within you that cause your inner conflict and confusion. Without self-awareness, the Inner Beings call the shots on your life without you knowing.

This is a key moment in your transformational process: meeting your Inner Beings and developing a relationship with them. Although challenging, confronting them gives you access to a golden part of you: your *Wise Self.*

Understanding inner conflict

None of us are strangers to inner conflict. It's the tug of war between head and heart, the quarrel of the angel and the devil on your shoulders. There are plenty of opportunities for inner conflict: it is estimated that we make 35,000 decisions a day, each with their own set of consequences. Life is constantly presenting opportunities, forks in the road; dangling carrots in front of our noses. How are we supposed to know if our choices are right? How do we discern the voice of reason from the competing voices within?

Inner conflict is the result of motivations, needs or beliefs that are at odds with each other. Sometimes, we feel pulled in one direction by a voice urging us that way, while another voice pulls us in the opposite direction: do you pursue your dream career or stay put in your safe one? Do you leave your relationship or try to make it work? Do you live a simpler life in the countryside or live in the city with access to everything? Do you follow what your friends are doing or listen to your heart? Do you have kids or choose not to?

Inner conflict doesn't just show up during times when there are big decisions to be made – it shows up on a daily basis. Should you get up early to go for a run or relax in bed? Should you say yes to that extra project or turn it down? Read a book or keep scrolling? Healthy snack or treat? Maybe you're cutting down on meat, but doesn't that fried chicken look delicious?

Too often, we brush off our conflicting feelings and thoughts and succumb to decisions that are dictated by our subconscious mind; we do what we feel we 'should', letting guilt steer our choices. We choose 'safe' rather than 'stretch' when we let our unconscious motivations make our decisions.

What's interesting is that we also *convince ourselves* that we are right in making our eventual decision. In psychological terms, having opposing beliefs and needs leads to something called *cognitive dissonance*. But your mind is sneaky. It resolves this inner conflict by shifting the weight of discomfort to restore balance, and make us feel like we've made the right choice.

A good example of this might be someone who loves exercise but also smokes. They're fully aware of all the nasty things that smoking can do to their health. They shift the discomfort they feel when considering the health risks of smoking to a reasoning of 'But I only smoke one a day' or 'I know I can quit whenever I want'. Looking after their health and smoking are, of course, at odds with each other, but in their minds, they're able to convince themselves that their decisions are okay.

Resolving cognitive dissonance in your life might look like staying in troubled relationships longer than their expiry date because you've convinced yourself that the person you are seeing has 'some good qualities'. It may mean staying in a job that no longer satisfies you when you're dying to break free and explore a new career. This might be resolved by rationalising that 'Even though I'm unhappy, sometimes I absolutely love this job.' What's really happening here is that we are avoiding the discomfort of change. We are shifting the weight of discomfort and trying to convince ourselves that we are making the right choice.

Inner conflict is a doozy. If it isn't resolved, it either leads to you making the same unconscious decisions over and over again or to an affliction called *decision-paralysis* – freaking out over too many options, becoming consumed with confusion and doubt, and doing *nothing* instead. We've all been there. We become too scared to make the 'wrong' decision, so we sabotage our own efforts to move forward through inaction.

I witness inner conflict often in the therapy room with my clients. They struggle to make decisions because it involves stepping outside of their comfort zone. As they work through therapy, they realise the changes they need to make in their lives, bringing up the voices of fear, doubt and insecurity – which they often find ways to rationalise. Through recognising the competing voices of their Inner Beings (as you will in the exercises below), my clients start to realise that they need to stop living their lives for others and focus on themselves. There's always those other voices telling them that they can't, that it's too late, or detailing all the things that could go wrong – but they learn to discern them from the voice of their *inner wisdom*.

I just want you to know that as you do this work throughout the book, you might feel agitated and frustrated. It's easy to feel this and think that these emotions are a sign that the work you are putting into yourself isn't working. Instead, know that these feelings are showing you parts of your life that need to change. Your feelings mustn't be ignored or repressed.

Inner conflict plays an important role in helping you to understand what is holding you back from moving forward. When examined with self-awareness and self-acceptance, it is a vital source of information pointing towards old emotional wounds or skeletons that need healing for you to move forward. It takes you towards a deeper understanding of your belief systems and the past experiences that have shaped them.

Personally, I notice my inner conflict arising when I want to do something for myself – like spend less time in the office or take time off. I feel guilty, worry about what people think of me and feel selfish, even though a part of me knows I deserve to look after myself. Digging deeper into this inner conflict in therapy has revealed an emotional wound: constant expectation from my parents has affected how I perceive myself, causing me to devalue myself, and my time.

Growing up, I had a lot of expectations drilled into me about becoming a medical doctor, which I knew deep down that I didn't want to pursue. Despite deciding to study psychology, my parents still grilled me for years in the hopes I would change courses to do a medical degree at university. A part of me wanted to make them proud, another wanted to follow my own interests. For many years I felt conflicted, agitated, resentful and guilty. A part of me was telling me I was a 'bad daughter' and would break my parents' hearts if I didn't follow their wishes.

I've carried this wound for many years, long after I graduated in psychology, and it has become evident in much of my decision-making. I subconsciously projected my fear of disappointing my parents onto other people around me: I was afraid of disappointing people so I continued to give, even when I was burnt out. Healing this wound (it's a work-in-progress) is learning to lean into the discomfort of disappointing others, and giving a voice to the skeletons of those painful experiences. It's a 'part of me' that I have to try to be aware of, every time it arises, because it prevents me from making choices that truly work for me.

If we consciously explore our inner conflict, a pathway appears. The competing inner voices that overwhelm us can instead help us to heal past wounds, cultivate a better relationship with ourselves and find wisdom.

Parts of you

Parts Work by Tom Holmes and *Internal Family Systems* by Richard Schwartz provide two models that therapists use to help clients recognise inner conflict and the interplay of different characters, or 'sub-personalities'. I think you'll find this really valuable.

You have many 'parts of you'. There may be parts of you that want change and others that resist it. There may be parts of you that are angry, defensive, critical and fearful; yet there are also parts of you that are brave, courageous and optimistic. Different situations bring out our different parts. For example, we may find ourselves patient and understanding with our co-workers and friends but impatient and reactive with our families and partners.

Where do these 'parts' come from? Our 'parts' have developed through experiences in our lives that have left a lasting emotional impact or wound. A critical 'part' of you may have evolved from situations where there was an excessive focus or pressure on accomplishment (e.g. expectations on competitive sports or grades); a fearful 'part' may have developed from situations involving rejection or betrayal (e.g. break-ups, failures); an 'ashamed' part from judgement or criticism from others (e.g. being bullied).

These wounded parts operate subconsciously. Let me give you an example of a client who finds he holds himself back from opportunities despite wanting change. Leo is frustrated. He observes himself shying away from taking a leap into a creative path as a designer, despite having great ideas and the full support of a network of friends. There is a conflict of two 'parts': one that is afraid of change and one that desires it. Using the feelings of frustration as a guide, we discover situations in the past where he has tried to take a leap of faith and failed. We explore moments where Leo's parents erred on the side of 'safe' decisions or told him that his ideas were 'silly' and disregarded them, discovering that these situations still subconsciously influence him, despite his authentic desire for change.

***

You may want to 'get rid of' parts of you that seem to be holding you back from moving forward in your life. Yet the underlying philosophy of parts work is to do the opposite: you're asked to develop a curiosity towards the different characteristics of these parts and to understand how, when and why they manifest. The goal is to bring these seemingly conflicting and disparate parts of ourselves together to form a cohesive sense of 'wholeness'.

It is also important to recognise that the parts of you that seem to 'get in the way' of you moving forward in life have been *protectors.* They have helped shield you from feeling vulnerable or accessing the wounded parts of you. There is a part of you that holds you back because it is protecting you from feeling the *pain* of past failures. This part is trying to do the right thing by you because at one point in your life, *it worked.* If, like Leo, your ideas had been called 'silly' and disregarded in the past, perhaps at some point this part of you felt like it worked out better to *not* put your ideas out there. It was safer that way. This part was protecting you from being disregarded once again, and feeling all the emotions that came with that.

We have to recognise all of the parts of us we don't like – the parts of us that seem to get in our way, that self-sabotage our efforts to grow, and yes ... create many of the roadblocks. They have all been 'protectors' of our vulnerabilities. Being defensive worked for you at one point in your life, most likely a time when you were constantly being attacked. Putting up walls or withdrawing from relationships was once necessary, if you felt unsafe. It may be hard to realise it as an adult, especially when these parts seem to work against your wishes, but they have all been created for a reason.

You have subconsciously built barriers to protect yourself. Understanding these different parts of you, and their motivations, is going to help you unravel your inner conflict and appreciate the interplay between your 'new' and 'old' parts. We're not here to judge these parts or get rid of them. We're here to show them some love, maybe for the first time ever, and to bring them into a harmonious family within you.

And now, it's time to meet them.

You have many 'parts of you' but we are going to get acquainted with four Inner Beings: your Inner Critic, Inner Saboteur, Inner Child and Wise One.

Inner Beings

The Inner Critic

Our Inner Critic is ... a drag. It's always finding things that we haven't done, or done well enough. Like a taskmaster or inner drill sergeant, it won't let up: 'You don't know what you're doing.' 'If you don't get this post right, you're going to look like an idiot.' 'How come you haven't bought a house and saved any money yet? You're wasting your life.'

Needless to say, the Inner Critic often likes to use guilt and shame for motivation. 'If you eat another cookie, you'll get fat.' 'You should get on with that before you get too old' or 'Is this where you are in your life, still?' Making decisions with the Inner Critic at the helm can see productivity sky-rocket – usually with the expense of a burnout.

If the Inner Critic had its way, you'd be ultra productive, successful, helpful and perfect at everything – a superwoman or superman. You'd need no time to rest because you're busy helping the whole world and making sure that you are constantly validated.

But the Inner Critic, although a pain in the arse, is also a *protector.* The Inner Critic actually doesn't want you to feel 'not good enough', so it's making you do *all the things* to ensure that you feel 'enough'. The Inner Critic doesn't want you to feel as though you are disappointing anyone or not good enough of a worker, friend, partner, parent or human.

If you dig deep enough, you'll find that the Inner Critic has emerged from times in your life when you have felt criticised, judged or neglected – moments when you have not been 'enough'.

The Inner Saboteur

Our Inner Saboteur is a bit of a jerk. When the Inner Saboteur is at play, you want to do one thing but instead do the opposite – or nothing. It's the part of you that presses the snooze button fifteen times so you miss the opportunity to start your exercise regime. It's the part of you that blurts out inappropriate things to scare people off, and the part of you that calls your ex after the second bottle of wine. It's the bratty one that likes to mess up your good intentions to grow and change, who likes to trash the party when things are going smoothly.

The Inner Saboteur often operates by making excuses, telling you all the reasons why you *shouldn't* do that thing. It can create scenarios that make situations scarier than they really are, amping up your fear response and wigging you out before you even try. 'Move overseas? How are you going to get a job? Do you want to come back with your tail between your legs? You've got it good here.'

Although our Inner Saboteur can seem like a right arsehole, it's actually another form of self-protection. The Inner Saboteur doesn't want you to be out in the scary unknown where anything could happen; it wants certainty, safety and security too – much like the Inner Critic. It's just sneakier and less controlling. It's not that you *want* to self-sabotage yourself – of course you want to achieve your goals. But the Inner Saboteur controls subconscious decisions that foil your plans before you even become aware you're doing so. It prevents you from moving forward by keeping you seemingly safe in old patterns.

The Inner Saboteur came about from early experiences of loss, shame and insecurity. Perhaps you had your heart broken, took a risk that didn't pay off, or grew up in an overprotective family that made the world seem like a big bad place.

The Inner Child

Our Inner Child is vulnerable. It holds the pain of our challenging emotional experiences, typically from childhood, but also from adolescence and adulthood. The Inner Child is often sad, angry, resentful and grieving as it holds the feelings and reactions of past wounds, hurts and disappointments.

The Inner Child often emerges via reactions in relationships, shutting down or withdrawing, getting angry or pointing the finger of blame. The Inner Child says things like, 'I feel alone, I'm scared, I'm afraid, I need love, I need attention, I want you to be proud of me, I am lost, I need help, I don't feel good enough.' It points towards unmet needs and calls to the unhealed parts of us.

The Inner Child can be difficult to access. Its vulnerabilities are often protected by the actions of the Inner Critic or Inner Saboteur – actions that prevent you from feeling lonely, lost, afraid or rejected.

It's important to note that the Inner Child and trauma go hand-in-hand – negative experiences that leave imprints on the psyche, shifting the way situations in adulthood are perceived. Past pain can make you hyper-vigilant to threat. You may feel scared, unsafe, anxious or insecure in situations that are perfectly safe. The word 'triggered' is a psychological term that has entered popular discourse in recent years. A person might be triggered when faced with a stimulus that causes an overreaction to a situation, often stemming from unprocessed trauma.

Have you ever felt abandoned or rejected when you haven't heard from a loved one? Have you felt the desire to 'hide under a rock' when a storm of adversity arises? Are there situations that trigger a deep sense of worthlessness within you? Do you ever overcompensate for feelings of unworthiness through people-pleasing or overextending, looking anywhere for validation? These are situations where the Inner Child is at play.

The Wise Self

How would you describe the concept of 'self'? In Internal Family Systems, 'Self' is explained as an undamaged core that is the essence of who we are, bearing qualities such as creativity, compassion, calm, courage, connectedness, confidence and curiosity.

The 'Self' is here known as the Wise Self: the part of you that is the kind, loving and caring force in your life. The Wise Self is the leader in the boardroom of our inner 'parts', the part that is grounded, patient and respectful. Think of the Wise Self as your cheerleader. It is your intuitive guide and inner support network.

We all have a Wise One within us who sees the higher perspective, who has faith, even in times of strife. It is the Wise One who takes a breath before reacting, who observes the sensations in the body, the racing thoughts and the impulses and takes a pause – acting, not reacting. It recognises when our wounds are being triggered, when the Inner Child is unhappy, and when the Inner Critic and Inner Saboteur are running riot. The Wise One sits on top of the mountain and sees all, with the kindness of the Dalai Lama and might of Beyoncé.

How do you know that the Wise One is present? You might hear words like: 'It's going to be alright, you've got this, I believe in you, you are amazing.' Imagine being the parent to your Inner Beings but, like, *the best parent in the world* – this is the role of the Wise One, to show up when the other Inner Beings need love. Think of the times when you were in the dumps and there was a part of you that gave you comfort, or times when you felt anxious and you were called to self-soothe. Think of times when you might have had a blow-up with a family member but chose to step away. After a few days, you were probably able to see that it was all a huge miscommunication. This is your Wise One in action.

Meeting your Inner Beings

The following exercises are designed to help you meet your Inner Beings and learn where they came from.

Exercise 1: Meet Your Inner Critic, Inner Saboteur and Inner Child

This exercise will help you understand the characteristics of your Inner Critic, Inner Saboteur and Inner Child. Write your answers in your journal, working through the questions for one Inner Being at a time, starting with the one you feel you 'hear' the loudest.

1. When did this Inner Being first show up in your life? What was happening? Where were you? How old were you?

2. What emotions arose for you? For example, did you feel pain, anger, fear? How did it feel back then?

3. How would you describe this Inner Being? How and when does it show up in your life? For example, my Inner Critic tells me to work harder, my Inner Saboteur gets in the way of my exercise goals, my Inner Child holds the pain of when I was bullied.

4. How do you treat this Inner Being when it arises? For example, I tend to ignore it, to get rid of it.

5. What do you think this Inner Being protected you from? For example, you might realise it protected you from rejection, isolation, judgement.

6. What needs does this Inner Being have? For example, does it need safety, physical touch, affection, clear communication?

7. How can you compassionately relate to this Inner Being? If you could say something to that Inner Being, what would you say?

Audio Experience 6: Seen (17 minutes)

Part 1:

This sonic embodiment will help you to feel through your relationship with your Inner Beings, and allow you to recognise the sensations that arise when the Inner Critic, Inner Saboteur and Inner Child are at play. It will also help you to process emotions from past experiences, such as grief. You will need your headphones and a mirror. You may lie down or sit comfortably.

You will also need a quiet space where you won't be disturbed during the audio experience or afterwards, as you reflect.

To access this audio experience, turn to the front of the book to access the QR code, browser address, or open your saved Spotify playlist: *Darkness is Golden: Audio Experiences*

🎧

Part 2: Reflection on the Inner Beings

This exercise is here to help you to reflect on your experiences of meeting your Inner Beings. It's important to spend time decompressing from the process. Use these journal prompts to write about your feelings after you've completed the exercises:

- What was it like meeting the different parts of you?
- What feelings or thoughts came up for you?
- What can you do to connect with your Inner Child more and meet their needs?

Keep a journal of your experiences of observing these parts of you over the next few weeks. Notice when there are moments of inner conflict, or patterns of behaviours, thoughts or feelings that stem from past experience, and pay attention to how you respond to them.

Exercise 2: The Boardroom

Use this exercise in times of inner conflict or when you have a decision that you are wrestling with. This is also an effective exercise you can use to practise listening to the Inner Beings and integrate them into a cohesive sense of self. The aim is to ensure that you listen to each Inner Being in an environment in which you adopt the persona of the Wise One, taking in the different opinions without judgement or reactivity. Imagine this exercise is like being in a real meeting at work where it is important to be respectful and inclusive of all involved.

Imagine all the different Inner Beings sitting around a boardroom table, with the Wise One sitting at the helm. How would the different Inner Beings respond to the dilemma that you are facing? Give each one a chance to talk out loud through you or write down their responses. Ask them about their needs, feelings, beliefs, motivations and desires in regard to the question you have or decision that you want to make.

The boardroom of Inner Beings

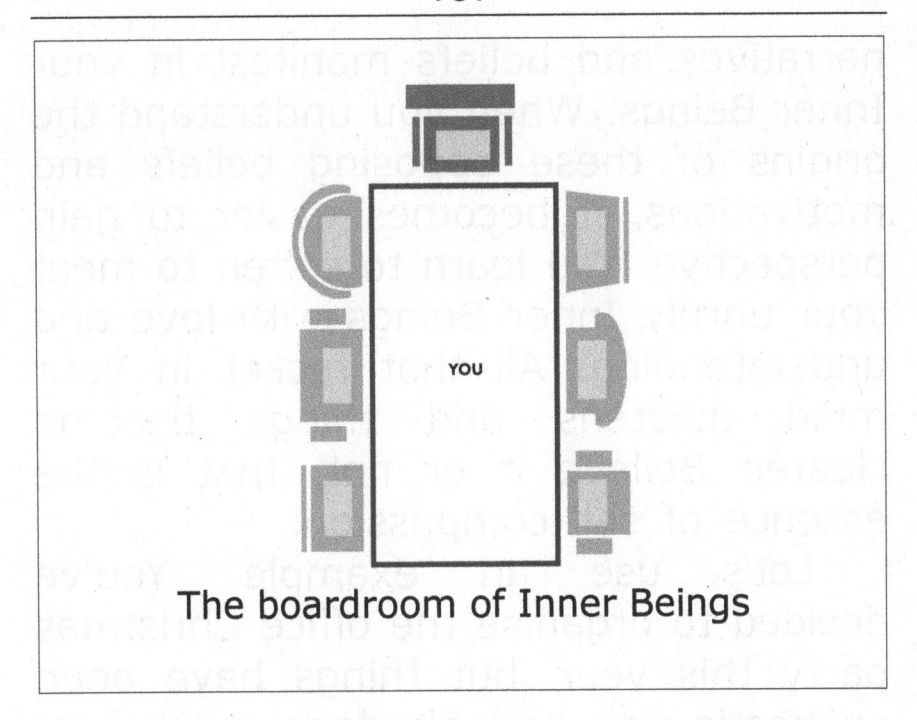

Self-compassion – from inner conflict to inner love

Self-compassion: you've probably heard all about it. It can sound a bit fluffy, but you know it's important. So, why is it so hard to develop, and how do we actually get it?

Self-compassion grows from recognising the source of your inner conflict, acknowledging your painful past experiences and the conflicting narratives you've developed as a response to them. These conflicting narratives and beliefs manifest in your Inner Beings. When you understand the origins of these opposing beliefs and motivations, it becomes easier to gain perspective. You learn to soften to meet your unruly Inner Beings with love and understanding. All that racket in your mind quietens and things become clearer. Believe it or not, that is the essence of self-compassion.

Let's use an example. You've decided to organise the office Christmas party this year, but things have been so hectic you haven't done much yet. One of your colleagues has offered to help you, with the best intentions. They know how swamped you are and think you can use a hand. Soon enough, they've put together a list of three possible themes along with decorations and costumes, and they've got a list of their favourite venues and caterers together for you to review. You feel your chest tighten. Your inner voice is raging: 'Seriously? This is *my* job – *I* want to be doing this.' You feel uncomfortable. '*Why are they being so over the top?*' You feel frustration. It begins to surface in resentment towards the colleague. Yes, the Inner Saboteur is at play. You've noticed it before, but this time you consciously recognise that you're annoyed, and you stop and acknowledge it. Why are you so frustrated? Is the colleague doing anything wrong? Or is there an insecurity that this is triggering? You pause and reflect. This *has* happened before. You like to take charge, as the validation you receive from people often cushions your own insecurities. You grew up in a large family and never got to be 'the boss'. In a sense, this colleague is robbing you of the validation you crave, the pat on the back you would otherwise receive by throwing a killer party. You take a few deep breaths, recognising the Inner Saboteur doing its thing, and sure enough, the uncomfortable emotions begin to ease and you accept help from your colleague.

Self-compassion can sound very 'woo-woo', but think of it like this: what are the qualities that you appreciate in a good friendship? Kindness, care, non-judgement? Self-compassion is your ability to honour *your* pain, rather than berating or judging yourself. You wouldn't ignore a friend who was struggling in front of you. It's important that you don't ignore yourself either.

Seeing and feeling the pain of past experiences by working with your Inner Beings allows you to open up to self-compassion for the challenges you've endured. It is the opportunity to meet the grief of the past and the vulnerabilities of the Inner Child.

When working with my clients' Inner Beings, there are often tears when they meet their Inner Child, as they reconnect with moments when they felt lonely or fearful. These sessions also allow them to express other emotions of grief, such as anger, shame and guilt, that have been withheld for years.

A central aspect of self-compassion is the recognition that *you are not alone* in your suffering, that other humans also experience pain, disappointment and difficulties. It softens the boundaries between 'you' and 'others' knowing that others have also had challenging experiences in the past that influence their present-day actions. As someone who has seen and heard thousands of people's personal stories, I can tell you – *everyone* experiences suffering at some point. It's often easy to judge others for their behaviour, but knowing that 'it all comes from somewhere' helps us to respond with kindness and love.

Exercise 3: Letter of Self-Compassion to Your Inner Child

This exercise is designed to help you practise self-compassion and is adapted from an exercise by Dr Kristin Neff, a pioneer in self-compassion research. If you aren't listening to the playlist already, this may be a good time to press play on *Darkness is Golden: Music for Reading*.

Part 1:

Write down a difficult experience from your childhood. How has this issue affected your life? What emotions come up for you? What are some of the things that your Inner Child might express?

Part 2:

Write a letter to yourself from the perspective of your Wise One. How would the Wise One respond from the perspective of unlimited compassion? How would your Wise One remind you of your inner goodness and humanness? How would your Wise One convey acceptance, caring, perspective and understanding?

To help evoke the persona of the Wise One, imagine a friend you trust who you can talk to about your troubles.

Part 3:

After writing the letter, take a break and make yourself a cup of tea or take a walk. Then come back and read it again, really letting the words sink in. Feel the compassion from the words.

Exercise 3: Letter of Self-Compassion to Your Inner Child

This exercise will help you to develop a relationship with your Inner Child and respond to its needs daily.

Find a picture of yourself as a child and carry this photo around with you. You might like to keep it on your phone – even as your phone's home screen background. When you notice any traits of the Inner Saboteur, Inner Critic and Inner Child arise, take out the photo of your Inner Child and reflect upon why these Inner Beings have arisen.

To do so, ask yourself: *What vulnerabilities or emotions are being protected? What don't I want to feel?* Take the time to express compassion and kindness towards your Inner Child for its feelings, thoughts and behaviours, strengthening the voice of the Wise One.

You are not alone

If getting to know your Inner Beings is proving challenging to you, I completely resonate – it was a crucial but painful part of understanding my own breakdown.

I'd like to blame my Inner Critic for pushing me to write for longer periods while berating me about how shit it all was. I'd like to blame my Inner

Saboteur for pressuring me to give up, triggering my breakdown. But the reality is that they were not to blame. In fact, they were working overtime to protect me – which initially seemed absurd, as all I could see was how they were contributing to my feelings of anxiety and overwhelm.

What they were protecting me from was feeling some of my Inner Child's biggest wounds: memories of disappointing my parents; times I had felt like a complete and utter failure; and the feelings of loneliness, shame and sadness that came from these memories. Thanks to my Inner Critic and Inner Saboteur, I didn't have time to feel those emotions. They helped preoccupy me with things like slaving over a sentence structure, only to find myself later mocking how pathetic it was, scrapping it entirely. Or trying on what felt like thirty different voices as a writer only to feel constantly frazzled and anxious – these feelings were preferable to my Inner Beings than the pain of past traumas.

The first step was just watching my Inner Critic and Inner Saboteur daily, gaining an awareness of them. It was clear that nothing was going to change in a day, and forcing myself to feel better would only make things worse.

I watched and observed how they communicated to me. At times I could catch them in the act of keeping me preoccupied, worried and stressed by simultaneously reminding me of everything I hadn't done and making things like folding the laundry seem so much more attractive. My Inner Beings loved it when I procrastinated. It meant I wasn't creating. I was protected from being potentially judged for putting myself out there.

Connecting with the Inner Child was the hardest. I wrote her letters, I put her photo on my phone wallpaper. I'd get glimpses of her and then I'd feel my protection mechanisms kicking in – I'd feel detached, distant and numb. It was all a part of the process – I wasn't going to get into Fort Knox without some patience. And then one night as I did my therapy homework, I lay back and visualised a conversation with my inner child. She was trembling and scared. For the first time, I acknowledged her pain. I held her hand and wrapped her up in a hug. This was the pain that had been with me, the architect of my self-beliefs. I got it. I could see why such strong protection mechanisms existed. Grief really hurts.

Feeling the grief and holding the Inner Child gave space for some long-awaited self-compassion. I actually started being kind to myself. It's hard to continually be a hard-arse to yourself when you experience your vulnerabilities so poignantly.

***

I know that meeting these parts of yourself is hard. It often means confronting your deep-seated shame, guilt and insecurity. But it is the development of these relationships that forms the basis of your self-worth and self-love. Through these relationships with your Inner Beings, you can recognise that despite what you have done or haven't done, *you are enough*.

The torch of self-awareness shines its light on things we sometimes didn't even know existed. In this chapter alone, it has introduced you to four friends who have always been there with you, whether you knew it or not, trying their best to shield you from harm.

They watched as you cautiously took your very first steps, unsure about whether you would fall, and they have been there for every other step since, walking with you through your pain, doing their best to protect you.

Even if it doesn't always feel like it, they're trying to help you. It's time to finally acknowledge your inner family and show them some love. They are only barracking for one team, and that team is you.

You don't need to do anything more or be anyone else in order to be loved. You don't need to fix yourself to be a better person for anyone else. You are not your reactions, your thoughts or your emotions. While your inner beings may disagree at times, you are not your inner conflict.

You are wise.

When we are wise, we can listen to ourselves.

And when we listen to ourselves, we discover what we truly need in this life.

CHAPTER 5

What Do You Need?

How to Listen to Yourself

You come to a creaky screen door at the back of the house that leads out to what once would have been a spectacular manicured garden. But right now it resembles something out of *Jurassic Park.* Enormous weeds tower above rows of plants that have wilted in their pots, shrivelling in the darkness cast by the shadows of the overgrowth. Mounds of wilted flowers and dead leaves line the mossy pavers that lead to the central fountain, now intermittently spitting brown water from its top. It's clear that this was once a special place. But these plants have been neglected, their bare essentials untended. They need some TLC.

We all want to feel as though we belong, that we are loved and seen by the people close to us. We innately desire connection and the feeling of being 'held' by others. Humans are social creatures. We desire an ability to express ourselves authentically in our relationships and to not be judged. We have needs so deep and innate that we cannot get away from them, and certainly cannot will ourselves to stop having them. The specifics of what and how much we each need might differ, but we all have in common the basic needs to be *seen* and feel *connected.*

From birth, we have innate needs: these can be physical, such as warmth, food and shelter, but we also have psychological needs: love, connection and understanding. And so it may come as no surprise that our parents or primary caregivers play a huge role in how our core beliefs are shaped – how we feel about ourselves, others and the world. Their influence over how we form our sense of identity and security comes from their ability to recognise and meet our needs in those crucial early years. These experiences teach us how to 'be' and what to expect in our relationships as adults. Can we trust people? Do we think that they will leave us? Are we loveable or worthy of attention? Will we allow our needs to be met? Can we feel safe and secure with others? Many of these questions were answered in our youngest years before we were even aware of them, so deeply embedded in our conditioning and psyche that we never second-guessed them.

***

Our needs are like the backstage crew of a movie: they might not get as much attention as the stars but they are the driving force that makes the show happen. When you ensure your needs are met, it is like taking care of that backstage crew – when they are well-fed, fulfilled and happy, things 'on set' work more smoothly.

Understanding and respecting your needs is key when it comes to helping you grow and thrive, yet often we fail to recognise that we even have needs, let alone know how to meet them. Understanding your needs is also fundamental to the health of your relationships: learning to communicate them brings you closer to people, allowing you to practise vulnerability and express yourself.

But we often shy away from exploring or admitting we have needs. We confuse it with being *needy,* or selfish. We deny our needs, which chokes our growth and happiness. Do you know what your needs are? Can you communicate them to others? Do you know how to meet your own needs? Now that you've met your Inner Beings and the skeletons of your past, it's the perfect opportunity to delve into the experiences that highlight your needs. In this chapter, we will be identifying your needs and laying the foundation for strong committed relationships – not only with others, but also yourself.

What are needs?

Your needs are essential building blocks to your wellbeing. They underpin your thoughts, feelings and behaviours. They are the impetus behind your actions – if one of your needs at a given time is 'support', you might feel motivated to call a friend, see a therapist or swing over to a mate's place for a chat. But if you repress this need, and pretend it doesn't exist, chances are you'll feel lonely, disconnected, and begin thinking that no-one is there for you.

In 1943, psychologist Abraham Maslow proposed that humans have five basic need categories. For those new to Maslow, the basic needs were: physiological (food, air, sex, water), safety (personal security, physical health), social (intimacy, friendship, connection), esteem (status, recognition), and self-actualisation (achieving one's full potential).

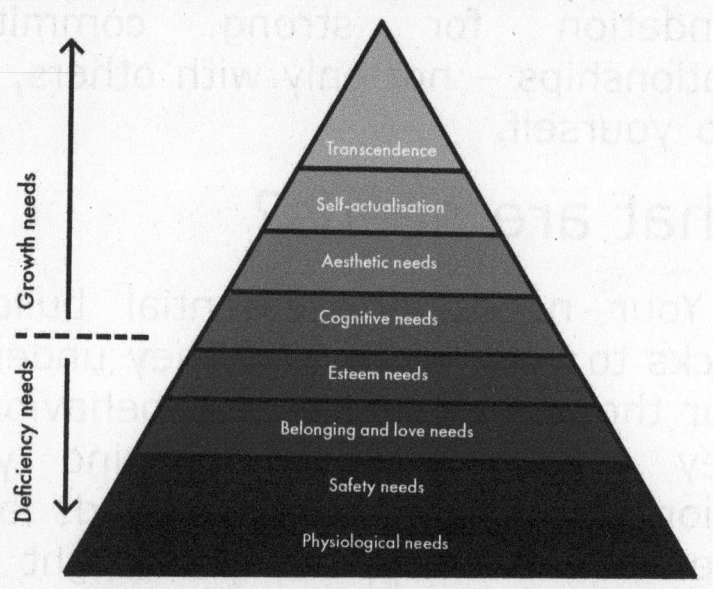

Marslow's Motivational Model

Growth needs:
- Transcendence
- Self-actualisation
- Aesthetic needs
- Cognitive needs

Deficiency needs:
- Esteem needs
- Belonging and love needs
- Safety needs
- Physiological needs

In the years following, Maslow added three more tiers of needs: 'cognitive (knowledge and understanding, curiosity, exploration, need for meaning and predictability), aesthetic (appreciation and search for beauty, balance, form) and transcendence needs (mystical experiences and certain experiences with nature, aesthetic experiences, sexual experiences, service to others, the pursuit of science, religious faith)'.

Whether you know it or not, your needs motivate everything you do. Sometimes it happens consciously, like feeling your stomach rumble and realising that you need food; but other times, your needs operate subconsciously. In a relationship, for example, you may have subconscious needs for attention or physical touch. The ability to be conscious of your needs can help you to tame unhelpful ways of meeting them. One common example of a subconscious need is a need for validation. Recognising this need could help you to realise that you are posting frequent selfies on Instagram to gain validation on a surface level through 'likes', rather than valuing yourself.

Since Maslow's model of needs came out, newer research has refined the concept further, stressing the importance of social connections above other needs. Social neuroscience researcher Matthew Lieberman and psychologist Pamela Rutledge are among those who argue that the heart of our needs is not food, shelter and warmth, as with Maslow's model, but actually *social bonds, social connection* and *collaboration.* Imagine Maslow's pyramid as a wheel instead, with connection at the centre of it.

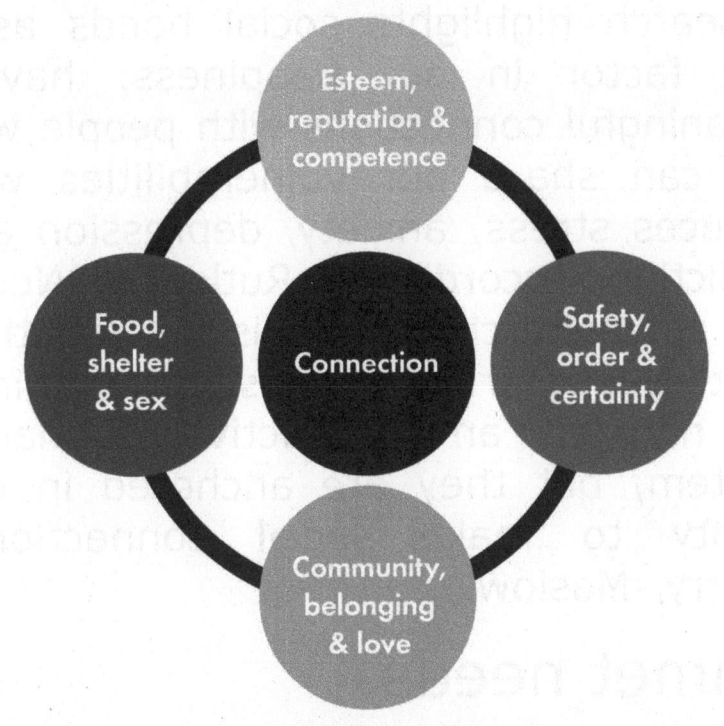

Pamela B. Rutledge's model of needs with connection central

Think about it: how can we meet our needs for safety, security, food and warmth without the help of others? How were our ancestors able to build shelter, fight off wolves, hunt for food and protect themselves without collaboration from other community members?

Our needs for social connections and belonging are apparent from birth. As babies, we rely upon our parents for comfort, sustenance and attention, and this need never really disappears.

Research highlights social bonds as a key factor in our happiness; having meaningful connections with people who we can share our vulnerabilities with reduces stress, anxiety, depression and addiction. According to Rutledge, 'Needs are not hierarchical. Life is messier than that. Needs are, like most other things in nature, an interactive, dynamic system, but they are anchored in our ability to make social connections.' (Sorry, Maslow.)

Unmet needs

An unmet need is like a plant without water. When we are watered, we flourish; ignored, we wither. You cannot deprive yourself of an essential need, or you too, will wither. As we travel through life, we are 'watered' by experiences where we feel connected to ourselves and others. These moments give us the nutrients to blossom. But difficult past experiences, where we are rejected or hurt, can create a deficiency of one or more of our essential needs. Fortunately, there are ways that we can be mindful of our unmet needs.

You've been watering your philodendron once a fortnight and yet it's all hunched over, looking like it's on its last legs. When you finally pay attention to the label you realise it's chronically under watered. Different plants have different needs for water, sunlight and sustenance – and we all have our own 'needs list' too. Unfortunately, we're not all given a label at birth that we can pull out for reference to cross-check our needs, whenever we're having a rough time.

In order to understand your unique needs, you're going to have to mine your experiences for clues, particularly those of your formative years. Growing up, it was your parents who first had the task of meeting your physical and social needs – it was their role to provide you with love, attention, affection, validation, safety, nourishment and security. Yet, even with the most attentive parents, and even with a roof over your head and food on the table, it was hard for them to meet every one of your needs, especially your emotional ones. Remember, your parents are messy humans too. And at some point, they too would have gone without 'water'.

When one or both parents are unavailable emotionally due to their own emotional wounds and unmet needs, it can impact the development of a child. Parenthood is arguably one of the most difficult rites of passage and understandably, our parents may have been anxious, unaware of their own needs, challenged with the emotions of a child or struggling with the demands of being a parent. All of this will affect the level of attention and emotional support that we will have received.

My clients are often surprised to learn that their needs might not have always been met by their parents, even if they grew up in a loving family and have happy childhood memories. What was it like for you? Maybe you weren't able to be vulnerable with your parents, or maybe you come from a proud family in which it wasn't acceptable to talk about the tough stuff. But at one time in your life, your parents were your predominant relationship – and in any relationship there are times when we don't get what we need.

Our needs are shaped by our upbringing, but also by other significant relationship clashes through our lives; being burnt, or feeling rejected in any of our relationships – sibling, friend, romantic, work or otherwise – can cause us to believe that we don't deserve to have our needs met. This takes its toll on our self-worth. For example, if someone once judged you for 'being too emotional', 'being needy' or ignored your needs for love, it might leave an imprint that could affect whether you're able to open up in future relationships.

When we're unaware of our unmet needs, they can bubble up, shaping our patterns of behaviour. Entering adult relationships without this awareness is a formula for havoc. Our deepest desire is to connect, but the way we go about connecting can look very different. Have you ever said hurtful things to someone you love or pushed them away, when all you really wanted was to be hugged? Have you ever avoided conflict or confrontation to 'keep the peace' but swept issues under the rug that caused you to eventually resent the other person?

Conflict in relationships often stems from one or both parties failing to identify and communicate their needs, instead getting caught up in details of a situation or how things 'were said' in the heat of an argument. We can fail to recognise that at the heart of the frustration, *there is a need that is not being met.* For example, we might have a deep need to be understood, or listened to. When we make this clear to the people in our lives, we lower the chance for unnecessary conflict.

Whether we've had difficult situations growing up or in gnarly relationships over the years, many of us are at a loss when faced with understanding our needs. How often I hear the words 'I don't know what I want!' in the therapy room. Truer words might be 'I don't understand my needs!' – and a lot of the time, if we haven't stopped to consider our needs, we just don't. Or we fail to prioritise them.

The following exercises are designed to help you through the process of understanding your needs. Be gentle as you discover your unmet needs and meet them with compassion and kindness.

Exercise 1: Discovering Your Needs

This exercise will help you to recognise your needs in various areas of your life. This list will change over time, as your needs shift and morph.

In your journal, write down the needs that you have, associated with each of these areas in your life. Be as specific and detailed as you can, as your answers will inform how you can meet those needs when you set out a plan for self-care.

1. Physical (*e.g. I need to do some kind of exercise or physical activity for at least 30 minutes 2–3 times a week to feel good.*)

2. Emotional (*e.g. I need to be able to feel low and not be judged. I need to be able to express all my emotions. I need to meditate in the morning to help me regulate my emotions.*)

3. Social (*e.g. I need to be around people who care about my feelings. I*

need to be with nourishing friends at least twice a week.)

4. Intellectual (*e.g. I need to be learning something that I am interested in. I need to watch documentaries on topics that I am interested in.*)

5. Intimacy (*e.g. I need to have affection and hugs from friends.*)

6. Esteem (*e.g. I need to eliminate toxic relationships.*)

7. Self-actualisation (*e.g. I need to use my skills and strengths to help others.*)

8. Transcendence (*e.g. I need to experience states beyond the normal/physical level.*)

If you are having issues identifying what some of your needs are, here is a list to help you. Using the below words as prompts to help you identify other needs you have, add them to the list above and complete this sentence: 'I need...'

CONNECTION
acceptance
affection
appreciation

belonging
cooperation
communication
community
companionship
compassion
consideration
consistency
empathy
inclusion
intimacy
love/nurturing
respect/self-respect
safety
security
stability
support
to see and be seen
to understand and be understood
trust
warmth
PHYSICAL WELLBEING
air
food
movement/exercise
rest/sleep
sexual expression
safety

shelter
touch
water
HONESTY
authenticity
integrity
presence
PLAY
joy
humour
PEACE
beauty
communion
ease
equality
harmony
inspiration
order
AUTONOMY
choice
freedom
independence
space
spontaneity
MEANING
awareness
celebration of life
challenge

> clarity
> competence
> consciousness
> contribution
> creativity
> discovery
> efficacy
> effectiveness
> growth
> hope
> learning
> mourning
> participation
> purpose
> self-expression
> to matter
> understanding

Unmet needs from past experiences

Some of your most important needs stem from your past relationships, such as your experiences in childhood with your parents, break-ups with partners or friends and significant conflicts with others.

Unmet needs from difficult past relationships may be interfering with your current ones. We typically harbour the pain and emotions from past experiences and unconsciously project our frustrations onto our loved ones. For example, sometimes you may *feel angry* towards a partner or friend, yet with deeper awareness you might recognise that your response is actually due to your needs not being met by an ex-lover. Your last partner may never have listened and always had their way – and the effects are surfacing in your current relationship. In psychological terms this is know as projection – subconsciously taking 'unwanted emotions or traits and attributing them to someone else.'

When you understand how you react to having a deep-seated need unmet, your self-awareness lights up. You see the things that you do to unconsciously protect yourself. You understand how you may be trying to have your needs met through ways that aren't helpful for anyone – like being passive aggressive, bossy, or even unreasonable.

Exercise 2: Discovering Unmet Needs

This exercise will help you identify your deeper emotional needs that result from your challenging past experiences. Its purpose is to help you to build more self-awareness of any patterns of behaviour, feeling or actions that come as a result when these needs are unmet.

1. On a large piece of paper, or in your journal, divide a page into three columns. Name the first column 'Situation from the past', the second 'Unmet Need' and the third 'Reaction'.

2. The next step is to identify and write down some challenging past experiences in the first column. You have already done the work of drawing these scenarios out, and can go back to your journal to track them down (Chapter 1, Exercise 2: Meet Your Skeletons). Think about unhelpful situations or behavioural habits you have in relationships, and the past experiences they stemmed from. You can write as many or as little as you

like, but it may help to start with three.

3. Think about the needs that were not met in these situations and list them in the column 'Unmet Need'. For example, a situation where you were bullied at school may have caused an unmet need of safety.

4. What happens when this need isn't met? Are there patterns or behaviours or feelings that arise? These reactions can occur when you are alone or with others. Write these answers in the column 'Reaction'. For example, a reaction to having an unmet need of safety could be: 'I feel insecure around people I have just met and tend to avoid social situations.'

SITUATION FROM PAST	UNMET NEED	REACTION
E.g.		(if this need isn't met)
My parents were absent in my childhood	Attention and affection	I sulk until I get what I want
Being cheated on	Honesty and trust	I feel afraid and close up
I lost my dream job	Security	I work harder and worry
Mum was critical	Validation and reassurance	I get insecure and blame others
My parents were unemotional	Ability to be vulnerable	I withdraw and drink
I was bullied at school	Safety	I get angry & defensive
I had a controlling partner	Expression	I feel sad

Learning how to attend to your needs

Now that you have identified your needs, it's time to learn how to attend to them.

Filling your cup is the act of replenishing your reserves of emotional, spiritual, physical and other needs. You can fill your cup through your own self-care, or with others through nourishing connection and communicating your needs.

Self-care

Self-care is not just bubble baths and face masks but rather the regular and intentional act of taking care of your own needs. Self-care can come in a multitude of packages: journalling, exercising, deepening friendships, carving out regular time for a hobby – or even simply checking in with yourself and asking, 'How are you doing?' This isn't indulgent, it's essential.

Self-care helps us acknowledge the parts of us that still may be hurting from past experiences.

You need to care for yourself the same way you would a friend or partner, recognising that you have unique needs. This is something that I have had to learn too. I used to think self-care was 'soft' and, to be honest, a bit airy fairy. But when I recognised that true self-care was a *conscious effort to recognise that I needed something* (rather than just an 'act' that I 'should' do), it began to feel supportive, nourishing and essential.

You give so much of your energy out to your work and to other people, it's important that you find ways to replenish yourself on a regular basis. As an entrepreneur and business owner, I've worked so hard that I've burnt out so many times over the years. I wasn't aware of what my true needs were, and I had subconsciously been driven by a need to be validated and gain respect, so I pedalled harder and harder. But eventually I realised that if I actually listened to my body, my needs were calling out: they were begging me to replenish the tank.

I now understand that I need slow mornings. I need daily movement. I need intellectual stimulation, deep chats, nature and lots of rest. That might sound really simple, but when I'm feeling off, there's a good chance that I'm neglecting one of those needs. I still have a desire to achieve, to accomplish and to give, but I now approach this from an intention of self-sustainability. I've learnt to keep an eye on the tank.

Your body is the access point to a deeper understanding of your needs. The mind tells you what you want, but your body tells you what it *needs.* To put it slightly differently, the mind tells us we can push harder, the body tells us we need rest. The more we are able to practise body-awareness, the more we are able to intuit our needs, but it takes time to find that connection with the body. All the practices that I am showing you, from your meditations to your sonic embodiments, are here to help you form a relationship with your body, so that you can learn to listen to yourself and find your way to true self-care, so remember to practise them regularly.

Practising vulnerability

When you are vulnerable with the people in your life, your need for connection is met. *Vulnerability* is defined by esteemed research professor and vulnerability champion, Brené Brown as 'showing up and being seen'. It is expressing what you really think, feel, want and need, without censorship, despite how others may perceive you. Yes, you may fall flat on your face, you may meet rejection, but you also create the possibility of being respected for your openness, of being heard, and of giving someone permission to do the same.

The type of vulnerability that I am talking about here isn't about going and asking that cute guy or girl out, presenting an idea at a team meeting or starting your own business. It's about finding a good friend and having a deep and meaningful, no-holds barred chat in which you bare your soul: what irks you, what's hard and where you're really at.

How vulnerable are you, really? Vulnerability has become a bit of a buzz word among woke circles of late. More and more we see people opening up about their struggles on social media. On one hand, these actions are stimulating vital discussions around mental health, and encouraging more people to open up themselves. But on the other hand, there is a limit to how much we are willing to share with our online friends or followers. And so, even at its most revealing, we experience a type of measured vulnerability.

Measured vulnerability ... is not really the point of vulnerability. Do you offer those close to you a warts-and-all account of how you're feeling, or do you skim over the details? Do you speak to them in the actual moment you're feeling down, or do you wait until a week later so that you can discuss it without bursting into tears?

What would it take for you to reach out and tell someone: '*I need you to be there for me*' or to say, '*I'm having a really tough time right now*'? This journey is about learning to fill the well of your own needs, but it's also about building the self-worth required to believe that your needs *can actually* be met by others.

***

Solid, heart-warming, authentic connection with another person is a gateway for us to heal our emotional wounds. It gives us a chance to *rewrite our patterns through the experience of healthy relationships*. It is an opportunity to create new positive beliefs, by showing you that you can have relationships in which you are vulnerable, and reinforcing that people will be there for you in your weakest moments. We need each other. We can't walk this path alone. There's no single person that is going to meet all of your needs – no therapist, partner, or friend. This is why it's important that you have a few people who can hold space for you, each meeting different needs.

Holding space is a term used to describe the energy of safety that we can create and have others create for us. If someone is holding space for you, they are allowing you to be yourself, and nothing else. In this space you can communicate your genuine, authentic self without fear of judgement. They don't try to 'fix' you but give you their full attention, which gives you permission to feel and say what you need to. When someone holds space, there is no expectation on you to feel or act any certain way. It's a gentle space, unfettered by advice, where patience, respect and love can live. It is within this space you can relax into being human: messy and real.

Recently, my good friend Anna was going through a rough patch. She would leave my messages unanswered for days, and send short texts every so often letting me know that she was in a bad headspace but trying to work through it. I respected her space, and after a week or so she came over for dinner. When you're a psychologist, friends often come to you for advice. But what Anna needed in this moment was not advice. She needed to be held, to have her fears heard, her anxieties out on the table. She needed to be able to fall apart and be witnessed – not problem solved. Anna eventually cried for what she said was the first time in months. She admitted: 'I have no idea what I'm doing with my life.' She had told other friends that things had been tough, but had been reluctant to open up on this level – her vulnerability had been measured. By simply being there for her, holding space, not trying to make it better, Anna was able to be truly vulnerable, to feel everything going on for her and share that with me. This is the glue that truly binds our human relationships together.

***

Many people shy away from admitting that they have needs for connection because they are afraid of being needy. Being needy is not the same as *having needs.* Being needy comes from a place of insecurity, where you expect others to validate you and make you feel better about yourself without attempting to fill your own cup. It's guilting people for tending to *their* needs, even though you aren't meeting your own.

Recognising that you have needs is very different. Not only do you work on meeting your needs yourself, you aren't expecting others to meet yours all the time either; in fact, you aren't disappointed when people don't meet your needs. You recognise that they can only give you what they can. When you are chronically not having your needs met in a relationship, you understand that you have a choice to discuss it, and a choice to leave.

The following exercises will walk you through the practice of self-care and practices of vulnerability. This is healing work – healing within yourself as you tend to your needs, and healing through relationships that give you nourishment and support.

> ## Exercise 3: Meeting Your Needs Through Self-Care
>
> This exercise helps you to identify specific responses to your needs that suit you, and that you can enact through self-care. List your needs (identified in Exercises 1 and 2) and write down how you can meet them through actionable responses.
>
> | NEED | HOW CAN I MEET THAT NEED? |
> |---|---|
> | Connection | Give a friend a call every second day; text someone every morning |
> | Freedom | Go to the cinema alone; bike ride to places I've never been |
>
> | NEED | HOW CAN I MEET THAT NEED? |
> |---|---|
> | Community | Join a group that has common interests, e.g. book club, choir, sporting team |
> | Love | Take myself out on a date; compliment myself |
> | Acceptance | Be compassionate to myself when I make mistakes |
> | Grounding | Meditate; exercise; eat healthily; spend time in nature |
>
> Commit to an act of self-care whereby you meet your needs every day for one week. For example, on a Sunday plan what daily acts of self-care you will enact for the week. Write them in your diary and set a

notification for them, much like an appointment or meeting. Scheduling your self-care ensures that you are more likely to keep your promises to yourself. If your needs change (e.g. you've had a busy week and you recognise that you need rest), modify your activity accordingly.

Exercise 4: Tuning Into Your Needs Through Your Body

This is a simple exercise that you can try anytime that you feel restless, stuck, frustrated or annoyed. It will help you identify your needs in that very moment.

Ideally, these exercises are best practised when you can be in a room alone with minimal distractions, to help you connect with your bodily sensations – but the truth is, you can't always access these conditions when these emotions arise. I have practised these exercises while sitting on a bus, or in a park on my lunch break, and still found connecting with my needs in the moment extremely useful. You can sit or lie down, depending on your preference. The exercise takes at least three minutes but can extend to ten if you have the time to go deeper.

1. Ground yourself by closing your eyes, taking a few deep breaths, and noticing sensations in the body. Take as long as you need – at least a few minutes.

2. Notice the uncomfortable sensations in your body, allowing yourself to feel your feelings.

3. Put a hand on the part of the body where you are feeling an uncomfortable sensation, and imagine that you are breathing into this space.

4. Ask yourself: 'Have I felt this feeling before?' and see if you can determine the root cause of this feeling. For example, you may have received a text message from a friend that has made you angry. If you have felt this feeling before, try to identify when and where. For example, is this the same feeling you get when your mum says something insensitive?

5. Ask yourself: 'What do I need?' Listen to yourself, listening for urges, words and messages that connect you with your needs. An example may be that you feel the need for physical space and an urge to be outside, or sense that you need physical touch in the form of a hug.

6. Decide how and when you will meet that need. For example, if you have a need for physical space, you might stop what you are doing, go for a walk outside, or leave a crowded place. If you need physical touch, you can ask your friend or partner to give you a hug, or if no-one is around, give yourself a big hug or take a hot shower or bath.

Exercise 5: Practising Vulnerability

This exercise is a practice of vulnerability between yourself and a close friend. Through this conversation you will share your challenges and struggles, and express your needs. This is the type of conversation that forms the basis of our connection with others – the glue. It allows you to fully express yourself, but also to be received, and creates a channel for that person to be received by you.

Decide who you would like to open up to by thinking of those people who you trust, or who have been vulnerable with you in the past. Be conscious of your gut instincts to shut down this exercise, or the little voice that says, 'They won't get it' or 'What will they think of me?' – this is your Inner Critic and Saboteur, both trying to protect you from vulnerability by igniting a fear response.

You are welcoming in a trusted companion on your journey. While this may initially seem daunting, once you open this channel of communication with a friend, it will begin to become more natural and form a more enduring form of support. Aim to practise these conversations at least once a week, with the vision of it becoming a regular part of your life.

1. If you are new to this, you can start with a text message or phone

call, but work towards having face-to-face conversations. You can start with: 'I'm going through a lot right now and I need your support or someone to talk to' or 'Hey, XXXX, so I've been working on myself lately and I wanted to share some of the things that have been coming up for me.' You can even let them know that you are attempting to practise vulnerability and let them in on your intentions of the exercise. This is an act of vulnerability itself! For example, you could say: 'So I'm reading this book and working through some of my challenges, like my need to be vulnerable. I've chosen you to practise vulnerability with because I trust you.'

2. Express an unmet need that you have (e.g. for support, connection, someone to listen to you). You might say: 'I've been working on understanding my needs and have noticed that I have a really strong need for XXXX and XXXX – but I don't feel like I'm meeting those needs at the moment.'

3. Share your feelings (e.g. I feel lost, disappointed, afraid). You could say: 'This is making me feel...'. You may be able to use a real life example of something that's happened as a result: for example, 'The other day I just broke down' or 'I've had really bad chest pains from the anxiety.'

4. If you feel comfortable, share some of your past experiences that you have been working through. You might say: 'I'm realising that a lot of this may be caused by...'

5. Notice your thoughts and what it feels like in your body as you practise vulnerability. It's okay to have fears about being judged, or of being a burden and feeling a sensation of discomfort in your body. Feelings such as awkwardness, insecurity, doubt, fear, embarrassment, guilt and shame are normal and you can even express those feelings.

6. Be mindful if you notice that you are engaging in *measured vulnerability* – holding yourself back, deflecting the conversation away from

yourself or minimising your experience.

7. Do not prepare what you are going to say: allow the conversation to have its imperfections.

8. Remember, you're not here to fix the problem – and there is no pressure on the listener to fix it either. You can choose whether to take advice or not. Feel free to let them know that you're grateful for the advice, but just having them listen is enough of a support. You might say: 'Honestly, just knowing I can share this with you means a lot to me – you don't need to have all the answers. I appreciate you just being there and listening.'

9. Don't stop at one conversation. Continue to deepen your relationship by sharing your feelings on a regular basis. This is the first step to deeper connection.

After your conversation, sit with your thoughts, feelings and behaviours and reflect on them in your journal. You can use the prompts below to help you.

> **Journal prompts:**
> • What feelings or fears came up for you before, during or after your conversations?
> • Did you find yourself deflecting attention away from yourself during the conversation?
> • What did it feel like to be seen, heard and understood?

You are not alone

I know how hard it can be to learn how to focus on yourself, to give yourself the care and attention that you would for someone that you love. While writing this book and grieving the loss of my father, recognising and attending to my needs – especially around connecting with others – was the lifeline that pulled me out of some pretty dark places.

It feels strange to say it, but I wasn't used to thinking about my own needs. I had built my whole career around helping others and it became an obsessive focus. The irony was not lost on me: in building an organisation to help numerous people on their mental health journeys, I was putting my own mental health last.

I was ambitious. My business went from a one-room psychology practice and a team of three people working around the dining room table in my apartment, to a complex mental health organisation in a three-storey building, with a team of fifty, in a relatively short amount of time.

Work was everything. I worked ridiculous hours, and even when I wasn't there physically, I was still giving it my emotional energy. I felt I had to: I had taken out huge loans to expand the business, and it was financially unsustainable. Seeing losses in the tens of thousands every month was stressful and heartbreaking, considering how much effort I was putting into it. I didn't want the business to fail and it only spurred me to work even harder. I literally powered through everything, running on adrenaline, keeping my focus on other people's needs and the success of the company.

The work took a toll on my personal life. It became very lonely and my tank fell to below empty. My relationships suffered – I was too drained to spend time with friends outside of work in a meaningful way. Friends stopped asking me to go out to things because I was always in the middle of a project, running an event, or too exhausted to hang out. Even when I was with other people, I noticed that I wasn't having fun. I couldn't laugh or have deep conversations like I used to.

I was a champion at measured vulnerability, showing just enough to seem human but never an inch more. Asking for help, being completely vulnerable and seeking emotional support was not an option. I was the head of a mental health organisation: I, of all people, had to have a brave face.

But that 'brave face' wasn't what I needed. My regular breakdowns, burnouts and grief kept revealing the same message: I needed rest, boundaries and time in nature. I needed to practise vulnerability and stop pretending everything was okay. I needed to realise that I had unmet needs stemming all the way from my childhood: I needed to be seen in my authenticity and be accepted for who I was, not what I did for others. I needed validation, but not in the way I'd had instilled in me as a child; by being hardworking and obedient. I needed to validate myself by reminding myself that my time and energy was valuable.

Through my therapeutic journey I've discovered that my independence and taste for accomplishment have veiled my deepest needs to be 'seen' in relationships. I've chased validation by working hard, striving and trying to be successful – all the things I *thought* I needed.

It's strange – I'd never thought I would say that over the past four years, I've achieved some of my biggest dreams, but I've also been the most dissatisfied and unhappy.

***

To be seen, I had to be vulnerable. I had to break the hard shell of the 'I've-got-this-together facade', and admit what I really was at the time – a mess.

I started practising vulnerability on the advice of my therapist a few years ago. The suggestion was simple: *let one person know how you feel.* I would attempt to write open-hearted text messages to my friend Krystel, but found myself writing and re-writing the text over and over again. I was judging it for being 'silly' and 'lame' and trying to perfect it.

I decided to let her in on my task, and explained that I was trying to practise vulnerability, which was a practise of vulnerability in itself. I admitted to feeling stupid, awkward and not being able to find the words to express myself. She reassured me by telling me that it was okay for me to feel how I was feeling, and that it was normal for me to feel that way. She also opened up about her own challenges with her emotions, which normalised my fears. She held a space of non-judgement and compassion, and since then I've built up to telling her my most hidden thoughts and darkest feelings. I've turned to her when utterly lost. And in these conversations, in which I was totally honest and didn't care about how messy I sounded or appeared, where I accepted that I was in a shitty place, I found relief.

It hasn't been easy, but meaningful connection has brought me back to life. I've gone from 'measured vulnerability' – just sharing a bit, but not enough to be uncomfortable – into the space of authenticity. I've retold and relived traumas that I've never shared with anyone besides my therapist. It can be hard, but it's *real*. I'm also not waiting for the perfect night out or a long dinner chat to share how I'm feeling. I'm opening up regularly to my close friends and creating the space for them to do the same. We've never been closer.

You may think that no-one understands you, but they do. The person you're opening up to doesn't need to have walked in your shoes or have all the answers. When you're vulnerable, and someone witnesses and acknowledges this, you feel seen and accepted. You feel like you matter. And you learn to subconsciously rewrite the old narratives and beliefs that say the contrary.

Despite what has happened in your previous relationships, despite what the monsters in your mind tell you about yourself, you deserve to be seen, understood and held. You matter. You have needs that deserve to be met. Rewrite the old narrative or belief that you are not worthy by taking care of yourself, tuning into your body, listening to your needs and responding to them. It may feel painful or hard at first. You may feel guilty about attending to your needs over others, as you've denied your needs for a long time. That is normal. And it's perfectly okay. You have been doing your best to survive. Now it's time to do what's best for you.

You're about to care for yourself in a way that you may have never done, ever before. You are acknowledging yourself and becoming aware of your needs; the foundations of your authentic life. You're seeing, maybe for the first time, how meeting or neglecting these needs has a huge impact on how you feel. The soil may be dry at the moment, but you are starting to recognise just how much water you truly need, and exactly how often you need a top-up. But without reinforcement, we can quickly leave our needs in the dark all over again.

Introducing your two new superpowers: boundaries and effective communication.

CHAPTER 6

How About 'No'?

Boundaries and Communication in Relationships

You've really dug deep to get to this point. When you entered this haunted house within yourself, there were so many missing planks in the floor, so many upturned nails and sunken holes, you didn't know where it was safe to walk. But you have been firming up those foundations with each need you've confirmed; you have laid and polished your new floorboards.

So, you're not exactly going to let someone walk in and scratch up your freshly polished floors after all your hard work. Now that you've discovered your needs, it's time to express them. To do that, you will need to develop the self-worth that confirms that yes, your needs deserve to be met by those around you. And to strengthen that all important sense of self-worth, you will need to begin setting boundaries and communicating your needs within relationships. In this chapter, you're going to find out how.

You're levelling up! You've met your Inner Beings and you're becoming more self-aware. You've found the skeletons in the basement, worked with your creatures on the ground floor, and now you're taking the grand staircase to the first floor, ready to deal with relationships. You'll be meeting another Inner Being on this floor – a very common character that we all play in relationships: the Giver.

The messiness of relationships

When life feels messy it's often because of the messiness of relationships. It can be hard enough dealing with your own darkness, let alone the addition of someone else's. We each bring our own way of seeing the world into our relationships, and this can be a recipe for conflict and flared tempers. We've played different roles at one point or another: the doormat, the aggressor and the peacekeeper. We've cried, fought, submitted and asserted ourselves in some of our closest relationships.

As a psychologist, I have a front-row seat to people's relationships, as they blossom and in battle. When people change, their relationships change too. When people become grounded, the wild waves of their relationships start to smooth out, or they find their way to calmer shores. The work that you do on yourself is reflected in the image of those who surround you. If you value yourself, you attract meaningful partners and friends who see your worth. It starts with you.

The good news is: you're doing the work. You're dancing with your monsters, skeletons and spirits. You're deep in it, fumbling in the dark, and building a light so strong that others can't help but notice it. You're understanding yourself: your quirks, your pains and your needs. It's time to understand the *you* that manifests in relationships.

Delving into the deep dark of relationships is another whole book in itself, but for now, we'll explore boundaries and communication, which are at the root of much interpersonal conflict.

Although this chapter is not exclusively about romantic relationships, the insights I've gained through my work as a psychologist for couples counselling apply to all relationships, whether they be work, friendship or familial. Working with couples who were unhappy and on the brink of separating helped me understand the positive sides of conflict – the gold that can be found in a relationship's darkness.

Most people think that disagreements and drama in a relationship mean that it's doomed – I've come to think the opposite. While never-ending drama is unsustainable, a relationship without any tension whatsoever is often one in which someone is not asserting their boundaries or voicing their needs, but instead being agreeable to keep the peace.

When the turbulence from a relationship is wielded skilfully, it can bring depth and closeness. When drama is examined consciously, it can allow us to understand more about ourselves.

Why do we get triggered? Are we having an emotional reaction that seems larger than the situation called for? Do we expect people to know what we are feeling or can we communicate our feelings? How do we communicate our needs? How can we grow from conflict so that we heal past emotional wounds?

I load my couples clients up with the same tools you're learning on this journey – mindfulness, self-care, vulnerability – which creates a space for them to express their emotions non-judgementally. Combined with a lot of patience, the couples that adopt these tools typically stay together. On the flipside, I've observed that the couples that continue to withdraw, blame or project their emotions without a degree of self-awareness, usually break up.

I've seen how a majority of issues in relationships can be resolved through people taking the very same process you are going through. In doing so, they understand what they truly need from their relationships, but also how to meet many of those needs themselves. It's a balance – we don't want to put pressure on other people to fulfil all our needs, but we also don't want to become so independent that we forget how to express and connect over our vulnerabilities.

With trust and safety, relationship difficulties can give us the opportunity to practise healthy ways of communicating that may not have been modelled during our upbringing. They can give us the opportunity to recognise some of the protections we have built up that are no longer necessary, like withdrawing from opening up, or being aggressive during conflict. Good relationships can give us space to make mistakes while we are learning to manage our emotions and triggers, and they provide the safety of compassion.

The challenge can be knowing how to recognise when spaces aren't safe for us to be our authentic and messy selves – and to realise when we have to walk away. This is where asserting boundaries can help: when someone does not respect your boundaries, it's a good sign that there's an absence of a respectful space for you to communicate your needs.

To help you to understand why boundary-setting or communication may be hard for you, I want to introduce you to another Inner Being: *the Giver.*

The Giver

The Giver – also known as the *People-pleaser, Carer* and occasionally the *Doormat* – is a common role I see in clients, and there's a good chance it exists in you. When we understand the characteristics of the Giver within ourselves, we can discover how to communicate more effectively and set boundaries.

Characteristics of the Giver

On the surface, the Giver looks like a Gandhi or Mother Teresa: selfless, helping, compassionate.

But at the heart of a Giver is a need for validation that feeds off being the hero – the one who responds to everyone's dramas, the shoulder to cry on, and the person others like to vent to or emotionally dump on. A Giver is a 'yes person' who takes on the responsibility of other people's feelings and wellbeing above their own. They often don't feel worthy unless they are helping and rescuing.

When you rely on external validation, there is usually an insecurity and neediness at the heart of it. It's unsustainable. This is in contrast to being internally validated – recognising our own worth and valuing ourselves.

When you take on the role of the Giver, the costs are heavy. You are unable to meet your own needs because you're caught up in fulfilling everyone else's. Your energy is not infinite; when you indiscriminately give your energy to everyone else's problems, you are leaving the pump running without replenishing the tank.

I once had a client, John, who came to see me for burnout. In our first session he said to me, 'I feel like I don't exist.' This was a huge admission for John, who was a creative in the public eye, and on the surface someone who seemed to be kicking all of the goals. As we went through this journey together, we slowly revealed that John was a serial Giver. He would overextend at his day job – working back til late, even when not expected to. He would smother his friends with gifts and attention and then feel short-changed when he didn't find this reciprocated. The catch? John was not giving because *he wanted* to give. Subconsciously, he was giving because of the validation he *received* in return. In those moments, with every pat on the back, he existed. But they were the *only* moments he felt like he existed. Over time, John had to tune himself into his *actual* needs, reel in his habits of overextending himself, and wean himself off the artificial high of external validation. Instead, he had to create more sustained foundations through self-care. From that point, he truly started to exist.

Being a Giver affects how you are in relationships. Some people might feel smothered or disempowered around you, while others may enjoy being coddled and cared for. It's hard to focus on yourself if you always prioritise other people's feelings above your own. But ultimately, being a Giver makes it hard to be vulnerable, set boundaries and have tough conversations, because underneath the surface you fear becoming a burden, hurting others or finding confrontation.

Do any of these characteristics of the Giver feel familiar to you? Do you find self-care hard because you don't feel 'worth it' or that you 'should' be doing something more productive? Have you felt guilty for focusing on yourself? Do you find yourself constantly busy doing things for others? Do you find it hard to ask for help or receive help? If you answered yes to some of these questions, the Giver may be at play.

Discovering the Giver in you can help you to identify when this character shows up in your life; just like your other Inner Beings, it is a part of you.

Exercise 1: Meeting Your Giver

This journal exercise will help you to identify characteristics of the Giver. You will acknowledge the cost of not attending to your own needs by giving to others unsustainably, and seeking external validation.

Write down the answer to these questions in your journal.

1. When do you think the Giver first showed up in your life? When did you start playing this role? And why?

2. How do you give to others? Assess how you take on the role of the Giver. Do you put others first or defer to other people's opinions? Do you feel energised or depleted when you do this?

3. What is your intention behind giving? Do you give to be useful? To help others? To feel good about yourself? To be valued or worthy? Examine whether your self-worth is connected to being a Giver.

4. What has been the cost of giving? Consider mental, physical, emotional, spiritual and financial costs. What goals of your own have you held back on?

5. Who would you be if you weren't giving? Do you think that you would be unimportant, useless, empty? Are you strongly identified with being 'someone that gives'?

So now that you've identified Giver traits within yourself, how do you reel in this Inner Being? How do you make sure you're preserving your energy for the right reasons? The answer lies in building your self worth and living sustainably. You can do this via two challenging but powerful practices: *setting boundaries* and *having tough conversations* in your relationships. ('Nope' I hear you say.) There's a good chance you go out of your way to avoid both of these. Here's why you shouldn't.

Establishing your personal boundaries

Personal boundaries are the guidelines that we set that indicate what we will or won't accept in relationships. They stem from having a solid sense of self-worth and an understanding of one's needs.

According to Edmund Bourne (an American psychologist and researcher on anxiety), boundaries allow us to 'separate our own thoughts and feelings from those of others, and to take responsibility for what we think, feel and do'.

Boundaries, like a spine, hold you up straight and tall. A person with good boundaries communicates *assertively* – clearly and with respect. This is in contrast to being apologetic and *submissive*. Asserting boundaries in your life might sound like this: 'I would love to grab drinks tonight but I'm feeling exhausted and need a night in' or, 'This is a lot for me to take in right now; I need some time to digest this; can we reconnect tomorrow?' In relationships, boundaries might sound like: 'When you make jokes like that I feel insignificant; what I would like is if you stopped telling them.'

Setting boundaries is easier said than done. When I work with clients who are learning to do this, I usually start by asking them what has stopped them from setting boundaries in the past. The reply is almost always: 'I don't want to upset the person.' It makes sense – who wants to hurt someone? But if we dig a little deeper, we can recognise that by making your response about the other person, you're actually avoiding responsibility for the situation. Nobody wants to seem like the 'bad guy'.

The truth is, you cannot control how someone is going to feel, nor can you base your actions around your prediction of what you think they may feel. What you *can* control are your own reactions and feelings. And you can also be mindful of feelings that you may be avoiding by not setting boundaries.

When I ask my clients what feelings they are avoiding, the most common answer is *guilt* and the *fear of being rejected.* Leaning into these uncomfortable feelings is an important path towards breaking the cycle of having poor boundaries. I want to be real with you: it may make you uneasy stepping into this sticky terrain, but the pain of feeling these emotions in the short term is better than the pain of not taking care of your needs for the long run.

In other words, most of us don't set boundaries because we don't want to have to deal with someone who's upset, but it's often our own emotions that we fear. I remember having a chat to one of my friends about a relationship that

I was considering leaving. I had been thinking about ending things for months, but something would always stop me. I remember saying: 'I just don't want him to be hurt', to which my mate bluntly replied: 'Maybe it's you who doesn't want to feel hurt.' In the moment, I was a bit defensive, but he was right. I was avoiding the pain of a break-up. Understanding this allowed me to *take responsibility* for the situation (and my feelings), instead of *externalising* the reason why I couldn't leave the relationship.

Setting boundaries is no guarantee that the person is going to cooperate. In fact, some people might not take it too well when you assert your boundaries with them, especially if it's someone who has benefited from your lack of boundaries with them in the past. This type of person has likely failed to consider your needs, or they expect you to be at their disposal whenever they wish. You know the type. They say things like 'you made me feel...' and become verbally abusive, indignant or passive aggressive when a boundary is placed: 'how dare you accuse me of...', 'after everything that I have done for you...', 'you would be nothing without me...'. Of course, how you communicate boundaries is important (and we'll get to that), but in relationships, these responses are often representative of someone who is needy, co-dependent, demanding or manipulative – and may indicate the relationship is not a safe space for you to express your needs.

Setting boundaries can illuminate where you have people in your life who are invested in keeping you small. It can be disappointing and hurtful when your needs aren't heard and respected, but this process also shows you where you no longer need to be investing your emotional energy. Often we fail to set boundaries and communicate our needs because deep down inside we know we'll get the answer that we're avoiding – that some people don't have our best interests at heart. The success of your boundaries is determined by your willingness to sit in the discomfort of setting them.

In order to create healthy and effective boundaries, you need to develop an understanding of your needs and rights. Boundaries will be different for everyone, but there are some basic rights that everyone is entitled to in their lives and in their relationships. These rights are central to your emotional and psychological wellbeing and are a great place to start when establishing your boundaries. The *Personal Bill of Rights,* developed by psychologist Edmund Bourne, can help you identify areas that you struggle to assert in your relationships. Have a read of them and highlight the ones that you have difficulty asserting.

- I have the right to ask for what I want.
- I have the right to say 'no' to requests or demands I can't meet.
- I have the right to express all of my feelings, positive or negative.
- I have the right to change my mind.
- I have the right to make mistakes and not have to be perfect.
- I have the right to follow my own standards.
- I have the right to say 'no' to anything when I feel I am not

ready, it is unsafe or it violates my values.
- I have the right to determine my own priorities.
- I have the right not to be responsible for others' behaviour, actions, feelings or problems.
- I have the right to expect honesty from others.
- I have the right to be angry at someone I love.
- I have the right to be uniquely myself.
- I have the right to feel scared and say, 'I'm scared.'
- I have the right to say, 'I don't know.'
- I have the right not to give excuses or reasons for my behaviour.
- I have the right to make decisions based on my feelings.
- I have the right to my own needs for personal space and time.
- I have the right to be playful and frivolous.
- I have the right to be healthier than those around me.
- I have the right to be in a non-abusive environment.

- I have the right to make friends and be comfortable around people.
- I have the right to change and grow.
- I have the right to have my needs and wants respected by others.
- I have the right to be treated with dignity and respect.
- I have the right to be happy.
- I have the right to ask for what I want.
- I have the right to say 'no' to requests or demands I can't meet.
- I have the right to express all of my feelings, positive or negative.
- I have the right to change my mind.

Setting your boundaries

We can all agree that setting boundaries and communicating our needs is an essential part of healthy relationships but when it comes to practising them, we often falter. Despite knowing (logically) that we deserve to have our needs met and that we are entitled to our personal rights, we can (emotionally) feel undeserving and struggle to find a sense of self-worth.

A sense of self-worth isn't going to fall into your lap. It is cultivated through practice. That is, the more you practise expressing yourself and setting boundaries, the more worthy and deserving you will feel. Think of the bullied kid in the playground. How does that kid feel when someone finally steps in to say to the bully, 'Enough is enough. No. Leave them alone.' When we leave our boundaries open, it's our inner child who is being bullied. When we maintain them, our inner child feels safe, protected and worthy.

To help you start out, it might be beneficial to get into the character of someone you imagine would have a stronger sense of self-worth. How do you think Tony Robbins feels? Or Barack Obama? Or Oprah? Think of everyone you admire. What would you do differently if you were one of these people? We can even practise standing like people who have a strong sense of self-worth and deserving, with our shoulders back and heads held high. Posture has a huge influence on our, and others', perception of ourselves. When you're slouched over, subconsciously trying to make yourself as small as possible, I guarantee you're not valuing yourself.

When I run courses, I get people to practise expressing their needs and rights to each other in pairs. They're asked to stand up tall and read them aloud, ensuring they conjure the feeling of worthiness as they do so. At first, they usually squirm and whisper the statements. By the end of the exercise they're booming, 'I HAVE THE RIGHT TO BE HAPPY!' and practically beating their chests. It's incredible what small shifts in your body can do for your confidence, and you can practise expressing your needs and rights in front of a mirror, watching your body language as you go. Give it a try. Yes, you'll feel like a dork at first. It's not supposed to feel normal – we're breaking the cycle here. But I guarantee that by the time you're shouting, 'I HAVE THE RIGHT TO SAY NO' at your own reflection, you'll be beaming.

Having tough conversations

I'm sorry to say the next part is just as uncomfortable but just as beneficial: tough conversations. These conversations will push you out of your comfort zone – they can trigger your vulnerabilities and fear of being rejected and judged.

We've all been in a conversation that has gone terribly: the point is lost, you end up in an argument, and you find each other bickering without actually dealing with what is wrong. Everyone leaves feeling judged, no-one feels heard, and someone is probably called an arsehole, at best.

In circumstances like this, adding some structure to the conversation will shift the dynamic. If you can, do your best to memorise the format in the next exercise: it will help you keep tough conversations on track. This structure works. It keeps you mindful of your emotions and potential judgements, and gets you to the crux of what you really want to communicate: your needs.

Exercise 2: Communication in Relationships

This exercise is designed to help you effectively communicate your needs and feelings and set a boundary in a relationship. The basis of this communication is to be clear, concise, non-emotional and non-judgemental, to give you the best chance of being heard and understood.

Using the steps, write out your version of the conversation and practise it with a friend. Notice the feelings that arise as you practise. You may experience guilt or fear as tension or tightness in the throat or stomach. It's important to notice them so that you're prepared for them arising during the real conversation.

Conversations can end in arguments due to blame, aggression or judgement. Using this structure will help you stay on track.

Step 1: Find the right time to chat.

You might say 'Hey, is this a good time for us to talk?' Or, 'Are you free tomorrow for a chat?'

You don't want to ambush the other person. When do you feel most comfortable to engage in a difficult conversation? For me, a good time would be in person, at someone's home or in a cafe, ideally at a time when I don't have to be anywhere else soon after.

Step 2: Describe the situation. Stick to the facts.

Be non-judgemental and specific.

You could start with, 'When you didn't show up yesterday...'

What is an objective, non-emotionally charged way you can communicate the situation you want to discuss? It's very important to stick with the unarguable facts here – do not colour the situation with positive or negative slants.

Step 3: Use 'I' statements to take responsibility for what you feel and think.

You could say, 'I feel/felt ____ (disappointed) because I think/thought____ (that our friendship isn't valuable to you).'

Avoid accusatory statements such as, 'You made me feel like...'

Step 4: Acknowledge possible errors in judgement.

You might say, 'I could be wrong in thinking that...' (Maybe I'm misreading things.)

Allow the other person the benefit of the doubt. Recognise your biases. Are there alternative understandings of their behaviour in this situation?

Step 5: Communicate what you need.

You could start with 'I need/want you to...' (I really need you to be there for me. In future, can you please keep me posted when you can't make it to things?)

What do need or want from the other person? How would you like them to change their behaviour?

Step 6: Try to find a win-win situation.

An example of this might be 'Is that okay? If not then perhaps...' (could you not make plans with me if there's a possibility you can't make it?)

How can you compromise? What compromises are you not willing to make?

Step 7: Allow others to have their own reactions and don't get swept up in emotionally reacting to them.

Take space if you need, or offer space to the other person. Take some deep breaths.

Recognise what emotional reactions fire you up. What can you do to remain calm when confronted with emotional reactions?

You are not alone

If this whole thing feels like a battle, I feel you. My therapist asked me the same question I posed to you: 'How do you give to others and what is the cost of this giving?' The answer was simple: I was the human version of the RSPCA – I was an animal rescue shelter. Instead of taking in animals that needed a home, I took in people's needs and fulfilled them – at the expense of my own. Even the task of paying myself a decent wage triggered the fear I was being selfish, so for most of my years as a business owner, I earned less than all of my staff, even the interns. It was almost comical: after working my arse off to build my business, I was too ashamed to pay myself more than minimum wage.

I want to be liked and respected. I want people to pat me on the back, tell me they are proud of me and have gratitude for what I am doing for them. But it has become clear that not everyone is going to like me, and constantly seeking approval from others has only caused me to devalue myself. Underneath the desire to be liked has really been a *deficiency of liking myself.*

The battle with boundaries continues; the prospect of having a difficult conversation with a work colleague still keeps me tossing and turning in bed the night before it occurs, gripped with worry that I will come across 'mean'; I've been pulling myself back from new projects; and most recently I've had to stand my ground with pushy landlords during the global pandemic. Despite the rocks of dread I feel in my stomach, I have the conversations I need to. Author and psychologist, Susan Jeffers was on the money when she implored people to 'feel the fear and do it anyway'. Asserting yourself is never really fun, but it's necessary if you want to wake up every day with someone that you respect – yourself.

I've discovered that the person I've really needed to set boundaries with is actually myself. These days, everyone is pretty understanding when I push back or communicate my needs – I discovered that it's often me who has the unrealistic expectations of being there for everyone. I'm recognising that despite what I do or don't do, that I'm still a valuable and worthy person. And so are you.

Know this: you don't have to take on family drama, be the peacekeeper or the one who puts out all the fires. You don't have to pick up every phone call and answer every message or email ASAP. Things can wait. You don't have to keep friends who don't reciprocate the energy you give them, or who load you with their frustrations without checking in on how you are. You can leave relationships or create distance from them. You don't always have to keep things to yourself – sharing a problem with a close friend doesn't make you a burden. You don't always have to have the answers.

Having self-worth isn't about having a massive ego or blowing your own trumpet at every possible opportunity. It comes from liking and believing in yourself enough to know that you deserve love, attention and respect. Your self-worth isn't connected to anything outside of you. It is a golden forcefield that is internally generated. If you think you're valuable and worthy, then you *are* valuable and worthy.

***

You are standing in the middle of this house and beginning to admire it. It's actually starting to look pretty good around here. You haven't turned your back on its abandoned rooms, you've stepped into them and claimed them as your own. Little by little, this is becoming a place you're enjoying hanging out in. You're proud of how the walls and floors are beginning to sparkle, how the dust has cleared from the tops of the furniture. You are going to do whatever it takes to keep it this way. No uninvited house guests vomiting on the carpet, no rodents creeping in and crapping on the tabletops, and no-one bringing their own dirt into the living room. You have house rules now. If you've ever had someone stand up for you, you know how warming it feels.

Now *you* are standing up for yourself. And that is one of the greatest feelings of all.

In learning to assert yourself by setting clear boundaries and strengthening your self-worth, you can forge a new path through the dark. That path holds the promise of authenticity, new exciting experiences and healthy relationships.

But to truly clear that space and replenish our energy, we must learn to let go.

And to let go, we must forgive.

CHAPTER 7

Breaking Your Patterns and Dropping the Baggage

How to Let Go

The next door is heavy. It stutters along the floor as you push, jamming. You have to squeeze your way in. Once inside, you realise why. This room is chaos – like an overflowing storage cupboard filled to the ceiling with suitcases, boxes, bags and piles of notebooks. It's a mess. 'What a dump,' you say, as you catch a whiff of rat poo. Looking closer, you realise that some of the books are your journals, the pages lined with the stories of your life, from your latest crushes to the outpouring of your heartbreaks, resentments and dilemmas. You shudder – it feels embarrassing to read about what you used to obsess over. Photo albums of every significant relationship in your life still lurk in this room that lives at the back of your mind: every ex, old friend and of course, your parents. The boxes are stuffed with moments you thought you had forgotten about, yet as you hold them, it all comes rushing back. Those moments have more of an effect on you than you realise. It's time to clear out the junk – your baggage – and make space for possibilities. It's time to let go.

***

You are slowly untangling yourself from the patterns that don't serve you. You are actually speaking up about what you need, and making sure your boundaries are known. You're opening up through vulnerability and understanding how this is the glue that binds you to yourself, and others. By exploring these challenges, you are spreading your light through your darkness and finding wisdom. Do you feel different? Are you expressing yourself more effectively? Do you feel any more deserving than you did a few chapters ago? Maybe you still haven't completely convinced yourself yet, but can you now see that the concept of valuing yourself is not just fantasy? It's a life that's very much within reach.

Through this process, you have the power to transform your core beliefs about yourself. And when our core beliefs change, our relationships change. I've seen self-sabotaging patients with a history of ruining intimate relationships with behaviours such as infidelity transform their core belief from 'I don't deserve to be loved' to 'I am worthy of love.' It takes work, but by valuing themselves, they then value their partners too. They become committed and their relationships deepen like never before.

I've seen a client dealing with the difficulty of making new friends recognise a self-belief of 'I'm not good enough' was creating a situation where she pushed new friendships away, always making excuses for why she couldn't attend social events. By transforming her belief to 'I am worthy of love', she began to engage, to open up, to share what she was going through. The quality of her friendships went from shallow and irregular to frequent, interwoven and supportive. In both cases, once these clients let go of past pain, once they transformed their limiting belief – their relationships became stronger than ever.

Relationships don't have to be draining, unsafe or scary but they can be when the Inner Saboteur or Inner Critic take hold. The skeletons creep up from the basement and spook our spirits. We become overwhelmed with negative thoughts and uncomfortable emotions, and boom – the pattern repeats. Until we drop the baggage.

Letting go is the natural next step of your journey. You've taken the steps to acknowledge and feel through difficult emotions connected to challenging relationships. You met these spirits and wrote a letter to the people who have hurt you.

This step also allowed you to be assured in your own needs, to know with confidence that these relationships do not serve you anymore. Little by little, you have been taking steps to release your worth within *yourself.* You are building your self-worth and self-love to know that you are enough without these relationships.

And now it is time to free yourself from any residual resentment, to open your heart. This is how you move forward.

Take a deep breath and acknowledge the fact that you are still on this journey. You haven't given up. That is huge. You're ready to spring-clean this room – and your heart – and make space for something special: a rite of passage. This is an essential tool in letting go.

You're moving into a new stage of life. This is the moment we mark your transition symbolically. You're about to let go of the baggage weighing you down, and discover the space of possibility.

The importance of letting go

Before we dive in, let's take a look at why it's so important to process, heal and let go of relationships from a sociocultural context.

Life has changed significantly over the last sixty years, and so too have relationships. Our parents and grandparents didn't have access to the technology we do, and their life priorities were very different from ours. According to Australian psychologist Damon Ashworth, before the 1960s, the transition to adulthood had two clear markers – buying a house and getting married. Mortgage? Ring? Congratulations, you're officially a grown-up.

These days we're more chill about getting married and settling down straight after school. Our priorities have changed – we now prefer to pursue life experiences instead. According to sociologist Andrew Cherlin, we've had an emergence of a new life stage called 'early adulthood' or 'emerging adulthood' between the ages of 18 and 29. Broadly speaking, these general trends are showing that adults in this stage prefer to work on their careers and personal development, as well as travel, before getting married (if they even choose that at all). As a result, we date and meet more people, put off long-term commitment and, on the whole, we go through more break-ups than our parents or grandparents who often chose to settle down young and have kids.

Technology has also increased our pool of possible friends and partners. We interact with more people, but in increasingly superficial ways. Our social worlds have grown larger, but we've replaced that much needed face-to-face connection with online interaction. Face-to-face interaction is important. It teaches us how to deal with conflict, how to communicate and how to be aware of each other's emotion. We've created new ways of talking to each other, but for all our emojis and GIF reactions, we've cut some of the necessary corners; we can easily shut down communication channels with people we don't want to talk to (i.e. 'ghost' them) or completely disappear from a cyber interaction. In modern dating, we can easily hop from one person to the next without ever having to have that painful but all-important breakup talk.

This has changed the nature of relationships. When I talk to my friends and clients about new friendships and romantic relationships, they are taking things a lot more slowly, taking their time to develop relationships. They are aware that no relationship is 'set in stone', and that people are potentially dating a pool of people.

In many senses, through these trends, relationships seem to have become more transitory, or even 'disposable' – if we don't like someone we just move onto the next. The issue is, each of these relationships is affecting us in some way. While many may be positive, some will undoubtedly cause emotional wounds. So, where does this leave us? We are having more relationships than ever before, leaving ourselves more open than ever, yet we don't really possess the skills to process them, particularly the difficult or traumatic ones.

Are you really healing from your past relationships? I see the standard formula for getting over a romantic relationship applied time and time again – we'll get a haircut, have a big night out, or jump straight into another relationship (sometimes all of the above, in that exact order). Even challenges with our friends and families seem to find little place for meaningful resolution. How many friends have you just 'drifted away from', uncertain about what really happened to cause the rift in the first place? How often do we bury our issues with certain family members, cut them out completely or just 'block' them? How many issues with workmates have you had to smooth over without really forgiving them?

Sometimes we prefer to run away from our issues, shut down or pretend everything is fine with others who have upset us. We don't want to take the time to really sit down and process our feelings. This clutters our minds and creates 'baggage'. Baggage is unresolved emotional turmoil from the past that we bring from relationship to relationship. It burdens new relationships with the limiting beliefs that *you* have formed as a result of your previous romantic relationships or friendships.

Baggage allows the past to affect your current relationships. It can surface in behaviour such as sharing less about yourself; refusing dates or judging new people in your life; overreacting to situations; taking your shit out on others who don't deserve it; keeping your heart closed and not trusting; neediness and the constant need for reassurance; being controlling and overly sensitive; being jaded and assuming the worst in situations. Baggage can stop you from being present. It prevents you from seeing people, experiences and opportunities *just as they are* – as potentially exciting, interesting, fun and mysterious. That is, the experiences that make life worth living. Instead you see these situations and relationships as hurtful, risky and threatening.

No-one intentionally brings baggage into their new friendships or bedrooms. And although we may never get rid of our baggage completely, it's probably better to enter new relationships with a backpack, rather than a tower of oversized luggage strapped to a trolley, ready to topple over at any second.

***

If you could visualise your baggage right now, what would it look like? A tote bag? A jam-packed suitcase that can only be zipped up by sitting on it? The lost luggage department at LAX? When I imagine my baggage, I think of carry-on baggage – a medium-sized bag that I pretend is light. It's actually well overweight, crammed with crappy failed relationships, rejections, abandonments and grief. The zip won't fully close and I've had to throw a jacket over it to hide just how jammed it is.

Imagine carrying your baggage everywhere you go: to a job interview, on a date, at a new book club. How does it impact your new relationships to be weighed down by these past disappointments and rejections? How do you communicate in a job interview or present yourself on a date with your baggage in tow? Not only does it hinder how you show up, but it must be tiring to carry this load, right? This is what you carry around every day. Its influence can be found in every corner of your life. That is, until you pop it on the conveyor belt to be processed and your hands are freed.

To truly let go is to get rid of (or at least lessen the weight of) the baggage you carry around. You've started that process by shining the torch of self-awareness on the relationships that left an emotional wound. You have recognised the impact of them on your thoughts (monsters) and emotions (spirits). To let go is to find ways to release the hurt, anger and resentment connected to a relationship that you know still affects how you feel about yourself, and to face the fear of moving forward. To let go is to find emotional freedom.

With less baggage weighing you down, you can authentically show up in relationships as the real *you* – not the one shaped by your past relationships; wiser, stronger and surer. You show up with a greater appreciation and love for yourself. You turn up holding the belief that you *can* be in healthy, supportive relationships. And that belief shapes your reality.

Letting go isn't easy, but you've been laying the groundwork for it in the chapters leading up to this point. You've engaged with the foundation of work that supports you letting go, and you're moving on to the next stage of your life.

I can understand that it might feel hard to get a sense of perspective on how far you have come on this journey. To do so, it is important for you to step back and acknowledge your path, to honour yourself. Ceremony and ritual offer us a beautiful way of doing this, and these processes have been used for thousands of years. It's time to support your process of letting go with your own rite of passage, to mark this significant transition in your life.

Rites of passage

'A rite of passage' is a way of marking that life and your role in it will now be permanently different,' says Dr Arne Rubinstein, founder of The Rites of Passage Institute Australia. According to Ronald L. Grimes, (professor of religion and culture at Wilfrid Laurier

University, Ontario), rites of passage mark powerful transitions, helping us to comprehend a bigger perspective of the human life cycle and the experience of transformation. He says, 'A transformation is not just any type of change, but a momentous metamorphosis, a moment after one is never the same again.'

Ethnographer Arnold van Gennep observed three basic stages involved in a rite of passage across different cultures. He identified these stages as *separation, liminality* and *integration*.

1. A **separation** is a safe environment or container in which change can occur – it could be held in nature, a therapy room, or just a quiet space from distraction.
2. The **liminality** stage is when the actual change takes place. It involves a challenge and the passageway of transformation.
3. The **integration** stage takes place as the individual is formally admitted into the new status. They then have the job of incorporating the knowledge that

they have learnt in the previous two stages into their lives. Integration allows the individual to recognise that an old identity has been let go and a new identity is emerging.

***

The Sunrise Ceremony of the Apache tribes, held after a girl's first menstruation, symbolises her path to womanhood and demonstrates the importance of rite of passage for the whole community. Over four days the girls are tested through hardships, testing their strength and endurance through dance. Every night the girls dance around a fire while the whole tribe watches, plays music and sometimes joins in with the dancing. On the fourth night the girls must dance all night, without stopping, as a symbol of the strength required to step into a position of leadership and adulthood. No matter how tired they are, they keep moving. This is a source of pride for each girl as well as the whole community. It is said that the song, prayer and effort of the whole tribe fortifies the energy of the community required for future challenges they face as a tribe, and transforms the girls into women.

The lack of appropriate rites of passage in the modern day causes a lot of confusion in our lives. Dr Rubinstein says, 'When these times of transition are marked, ritualised, witnessed, and supported, it creates a kind of experiential map of self-development. Without proper rites of passage, people can become disoriented and lose their way on life's journey.'

Despite their absence in the modern world, Professor Grimes' research suggests that there's been a huge resurgence in interest in rites of passage over the last ten years, as people search for meaning more than ever. His work is focused on the power that modern-day ritual and ceremony hold, to come to terms with life-changing events. When there is great change or upheaval in life, contemporary rites of passage can help process the associated stress and emotions. To respond to the interest in modern rites of passage, Grimes has created contemporary rites of passage for the arrival of menopause, cross-cultural weddings, same-sex marriages, blended families, divorces, adoptions, and helping terminally ill people who have decided to end their own life.

The ending of any significant relationship, marriage, friendship or otherwise, can be signified through rite of passage. This process can allow you to symbolically let go of pain, fear of the unknown future, and help to find new ways of being in the world. This is your equivalent of the all-night Apache dance. It is a challenge. You will need determination. But it will be a necessary process to allow for you to authentically let go, drop the baggage, and make space for a different future.

A modern ceremony for letting go

Imagine if you could enter a world that was created for the sole purpose of helping cut you away from the shackles of relationship pain. A space where you could symbolically draw a line in the sand and find the steps to move forward.

Transience – A Ceremony For Letting Go of Past Relationships is a rite of passage I created for one of my courses held at Indigo, *Kickstart Your Heart,* and then later remodelled for a public art installation at the Art Gallery of New South Wales. I recognised the need for a respectful, appropriate rite of passage in consideration of the way modern society sees us exiting more relationships than ever before. I felt that people needed a way to deal with their emotional burdens. I couldn't find any contemporary rites of passage available to help people let go of their pain as a community, and be witnessed in their change.

Halfway through the course I invited participants to come to the next session dressed in black. They were asked to bring representations of their 'baggage' – photos, soft toys, clothes, engagement bands, wedding memorabilia and letters that they had written during the previous weeks of the course. The setting was a makeshift 'church' filled with candles ... and a coffin. I had created a funeral, a symbolic reminder of the death of their relationship. It was a bit of a shock for these people to turn up for a course to find a candle-lit coffin in the middle of a room, but it was a moment I didn't want them to forget.

The ceremony involved a closed-eye sonic embodiment, to move each person through a passage of transformation. But this wasn't a passive experience. They were challenged to use this moment to forgive the person that hurt them.

Forgiveness is a vital part of letting go. It is the *conscious decision to let go of the resentment and pain of a situation or relationship.* You might think that forgiveness involves another person standing in front of you, where you have an awkward conversation exchanging apologies. But no, this process can be done even if you haven't had any contact with the other person in years.

I want to stress that forgiveness doesn't make what happened okay. It doesn't mean that what happened wasn't hurtful, or that it was right. This type of forgiveness is not about absolving the other for what they did, it is about unburdening the pain of the emotions that you carry. Forgiveness is for *you*.

To illustrate this, take a moment to remember a time when you were hurt in a relationship.

Pay attention to your body. Do you notice any pain, perhaps a tightening around your chest, heart or stomach? If so, this might suggest you're holding onto unresolved hurt, pain and resentment that is causing harm to *you*. You are the first recipient of your emotions. As you remember, emotions are felt in the body. When you harbour negative feelings, you feel them first. Imagine what it would be like if you didn't have to carry that pain.

Forgiveness is hard. I've seen people learn to let go of hurt from all different types of relationships, and the strength and vulnerability that entails. It takes a considerable effort to let go as you switch between holding onto your pain and the story of what happened, the fear of actually letting go, and then the freedom and lightness that comes with the embodiment of letting go. It's a process, but one that you are capable of going through.

When I held *Transience* at the Art Gallery of NSW, it was touching to see people move through this ceremony together, in a space lined with Andy Warhol paintings. Young and old shedding tears, shedding skins, creating space in their lives for a different way of living and being. Though the group were mostly strangers to each other, I was amazed at the willingness of hundreds of people to participate in the public ceremony. It reminded me of how imperative rites of passage are for our times. We all need safe community spaces where we can let go, witness each other, and know that we're not alone in trying to unburden ourselves from the pain that we carry. Everyone is carrying something.

Running this ceremony had been nerve-racking – I was unsure how it had would be received in a public forum, coffin and all. The morning after the ceremony I awoke to an email from a member of renowned Buddhist teacher

Thich Nhat Hanh's Plum Village monastery. Unbeknown to me, they had sat through *Transience* and were now writing to tell me they had been deeply moved by the experience. They acknowledged how significant the process of letting go was, if we are to move forward. And you now have an opportunity to undertake that same process.

By letting go through ritual practises we can symbolically mark a new stage of our lives and sow the seeds for our next chapter.

Are you ready to let go?

Audio Experience 7: Transience – A Ceremony for Letting Go of Past Relationships (15 minutes)

This sonic embodiment has been designed to help you create your own rite of passage to symbolically let go of a relationship that no longer serves you.

Make this ceremony special by creating an atmosphere that will help you to remember the experience when you look back upon it. This might be by wearing black and lighting a candle. You may like to decorate or place a rug down – anything that changes this space from how it regularly looks. Get creative and use your imagination.

Note that you don't have to have a spare coffin in your attic to hold this ceremony, but you will need a smartphone, headphones, a candle, some matches. You'll also need the purge letters you created in Chapter 3.

Find a quiet space where you won't be disturbed for at least an hour.

Step 1: Create your ceremony space: dim the lighting, light your candle, get changed into your 'ceremonial' clothes.

Step 2: Put your headphones on, place your phone over the QR code at the start of the book to find the sonic embodiment *Transience* in your playlist.

Step 3: Lie down and listen to *Transience*.

Step 4: After the audio experience, complete the ceremony by safely burning the letter you had written to this person. You may need to do this outside, depending on where you live. If you prefer, you can rip up the letter, or submerge it in water, and then throw it away.

Step 5: When you feel ready, share your experience with a trusted friend. Let them know what you are leaving behind and envisioning for the future.

Exercise 2: Forgive and Flourish

While the audio experience is recommended, if you are unable to listen to it, this exercise will help you experience the benefits of the rite of passage through the practice of forgiveness. You will need a candle, matches, your purge letter from Chapter 3, a journal and pen.

Write down the answers to these questions in your journal:

1. Who is the person you are trying to forgive?

2. What is the incident that happened?

3. How did it make you feel?

4. In your own words, and in your own way, write down the words you would use to forgive that person. Imagine that they are standing right in front of you and write the exact words you would say to them.

5. Afterwards, complete the ceremony by safely burning the letter you had written to this person and when you feel ready, share your experience with a trusted friend. Let them know what you are leaving behind and envisioning for the future.

Exercise 3: Aftercare

These simple exercises are designed to help guide you further in the process of letting go.

Part A – Physical detox

This exercise ensures that you are letting go on a level that ensures you are not resurfacing past hurts through your online habits, physical space or social activities.

1. Challenge yourself to get rid of things that remind you of past relationships that you are letting go of (old mementos, ticket stubs, gifts, photos).

2. Are there people that you need to 'unfriend' or 'unfollow' on social media?

3. Are there any new boundaries that you need to set?

Part B – Self-compassion Exercise

Understandably, letting go can leave you feeling raw and empty. This exercise is designed to help you evoke your Wise Self to offer comfort and connection.

1. Consider a person that has hurt you, who you would like to focus on.

2. Are there words that you needed to hear from this person that you never received? Take some time to write down the words you needed to hear from them, the things you wish they had said. You may find this challenging, so go easy; be gentle on yourself.

3. Stand or sit in front of a mirror. It's time to repeat those very words to yourself, looking yourself in the eye.

4. Notice what it feels like in your body as you do this exercise; notice if tension, emotions or resistance arises.

5. Journal about your emotions and experience: what feelings came up for you? Could you speak to yourself compassionately?

Part C – Self-forgiveness mantra

The *Ho'oponopono* is a Hawaiian prayer of forgiveness, a mantra that you can repeat to yourself to aid in the process of self-forgiveness. I recommend at least twenty repetitions (one after another), said out loud, and if possible, while looking in the mirror. If you'd like, you can try this practice once a day for a week, and observe the effect that it has on you.

'*I'm sorry, please forgive me, thank you, I love you.*'

You are not alone

While writing this book, I went through my own process of letting go. Because my father had died, I was discovering that I was processing the loss of the relationship in waves – emotions would come and go, some days I felt I could let go and see my future clearly, at times I couldn't let go of the belief that the world was an unfair place to be in because of the pain that I was feeling.

What was illuminating was that grieving the loss of my father, and having an emotional breakdown, brought up beliefs and relationships that I had not anticipated. It revealed skeletons I had initially not thought of – like my relationship with my mother, and my first relationship at fourteen, which had both left emotional wounds I had to face.

My first relationship came up in a therapy session where I was feeling very anxious and helpless. I assumed it was because of my grief. In the session we went through a practice of tuning into my needs through my body (see Chapter 5, Exercise 4). Feeling the pain in my chest, I asked myself if I had felt this feeling before. A memory from my first relationship arose. It wasn't a pleasant memory – it was a memory of feeling overwhelmed, helpless and anxious because my boyfriend at the time had tried to hurt himself in front of me.

***

At fourteen I was in an emotionally abusive relationship for two years. I didn't get hit or called names; it was words and actions that were the weapons. I'd lost myself in that relationship, and it all started when I began to doubt myself.

Things weren't feeling right; Dave was never where he was supposed to be. His phone would be off, or he wouldn't pick up, and his excuses started to not line up. I would question him, and he would always tell me that I was being 'paranoid' or 'silly' for thinking strange things, so I stopped, shutting down the nagging feeling in my gut, the intuition that was telling me that something was up. I was starting to lose the thread to 'me', my inner compass that would gently nudge me in the right way when I went astray.

A year into the relationship I found out that he wasn't just cheating on me, I was the second girlfriend. He'd had a girlfriend the whole time. My gut was right about the times I'd felt things amiss, but by that stage, that inner guidance was lost to me, buried underneath all the times I'd not listened, ignored, and turned away from it.

I'd wanted to leave the relationship, and tried, but things got really dark when I attempted to; he pulled out a gun, and pointed it at himself. We were at his house, in his bedroom. He then put the gun against my cheek, the cold metal resting against my face – I can still feel the chill of it now. What was I to do? Walk away? Stay and hope that things would get better? Either way, it felt as though I was destined to lose. I stayed.

Everything tumbled into this horrible pattern: when I'd try to leave the relationship, he'd try and hurt himself, and it would always be in front of me, so I would have to try to save him. Over and over again, for a year. He'd try everything, pulling out knives, attempting to ingest poisons, punching himself repeatedly and having uncontrollable manic fits. He never was serious about hurting himself, all he wanted was for me to stay in the relationship, but at the time I didn't know any better and it was exhausting, completely screwing with my head.

I didn't 'think things through', or have a chat to someone about it; I just buried it all and continued with life as if everything was normal. I still went to class, did my homework and started to get ready for my final years of high school.

Looking back, I didn't want to acknowledge that anything was wrong. I was in denial. And in the same way that the relationship had started, when everything moved so quickly, it abruptly ended. I went away overseas for a 'holiday', and when I came back, I had gathered enough value in myself to call it off. He didn't put up a fight, and I slunk away. I couldn't even call it a victory. I was sixteen.

The relationship was over, but not the wounding. At the time, I buried it, suppressed it and barely looked back, but within me, the seeds of doubt started to grow: How was I supposed to trust anyone? What was love? Is this what a real relationship was?

Without the tools to process what happened, the tentacles of this relationship found their way into others, strangling them. The patterns emerged: of not wanting to open my heart, not trusting others, not trusting myself, not wanting to feel, not wanting to get hurt. This set the scene for a lot of relationship drama. This was the distraction that I was subconsciously looking for so I didn't have to do the inner work. If that didn't stop me from facing myself, that role was played by other self-sabotaging behaviours: not respecting my body, abusing drugs and alcohol, and hating myself.

***

This was the relationship I had to let go of. When I wrote my purge letter to my ex, only recently, I surprised myself at how emotional I was – I couldn't believe how much grief and resentment I was still holding onto.

I held a letting go ceremony with a friend, to acknowledge and surrender the pain of this relationship. We created a simple ceremony, lighting candles, burning sage and listening to the recording of *Transience*. Afterwards, we burnt our letters, went for a swim in the ocean and talked about what we wanted to bring into our lives. I felt immediately lighter.

These days, whenever I've found myself thinking about that unhealthy relationship, I'm able to return to the memory of the ceremony and the conscious decision I made to move forward in my life. It doesn't guarantee that I'll never feel upset about it, but the memory of the rite of passage helps me to acknowledge that I am a different person, that I have grown from that experience and am not defined by it. After going through this process, I bought myself a small abstract painting by a local artist that sits in my living room. It reminds me every day that I am in a new stage of my life.

I have found that self-compassion supports this process of letting go; the ability for me to stop and tell myself, 'It's okay for you to feel what you are feeling', and comfort myself. If you find yourself being critical for going back to old feelings and thoughts, you can instead tell yourself, 'It's going to be okay, I understand what you are going through, I am here for you.'

***

A rite of passage is not a magical cure. It does not mean that we never relapse into old stories and behaviours. It is a memory-stamp, like a first kiss or first overseas adventure; it's an indelible imprint on your mind, of your decision to choose yourself and have a perspective on pain that is empowering, that you can return to when you wobble. Harnessing the power of rite of passage opens up a space for you to make choices.

I want to reassure you, though. If you aren't ready to let go, that's okay. We all become ready at different stages.

Sometimes, we are still in grieving and it's not the right time. There can't be a rush to let go. We cannot side-step sitting with our pain, and to do this is to skip an essential part of transformational healing, to create the illusion of healing rather than truly resolving our hurt.

I have also been in the process of unravelling my relationship with my mother, learning to slowly open up to memories of the lack of emotional bond I had with her, understanding my insecurities and anxieties as a result of that relationship and feeling the grief I still hold. It has been a long process of healing from this relationship, and I recognise I'm still in the process of holding space for my grief and not ready to explore forgiveness. It's okay if you are in the same place. It doesn't mean that you can't move forward.

Let go when you are ready, and in the amount that you feel comfortable with. Come back time and time again to your inner voice, which says *'let's sit and feel this'*, or *'it's time to let this go'*. Learn to see the cycles of these voices within you, and how they are showing you the changes that are happening within.

Like a hermit crab leaving its shell for a new home, we let go of the weight of painful memories to make space for new beginnings. It is a vulnerable in-between, leaving one shell for another, as we scurry naked to our next dream. Yet we'd understand the necessity of our departure if we were to look over our shoulders to see what we were leaving behind. Our baggage, the collection of our unhelpful patterns, nicks and cuts, lie in a heap in our old shell. It is what has kept us bogged down and burdened; it is what must be relinquished for us to find a new home, a path shaped by our values and needs.

***

Throughout this book, you have been working your way through the dark rooms of your house, the darkness inside yourself. It's been hard to see, but the light has become brighter with each step, as your torch of self awareness has grown more brilliant. Through the symbolic process of letting go, you are lighting a fire. Into the flames go the relationships that no longer serve you, and while they burn, the fire keeps you warm – it reminds you that you *have* let go, that you *can* move forward.

As you unpack your painful experiences and memories, no matter how crushing they seem, no matter how much the patterns seem to repeat, you are moving not in a circle but a spiral, upwards and outwards. From dark to gold, to dark to gold, creating galaxies of illumination.

Under the light of these galaxies may you dance all night.

CHAPTER 8

Mining the Darkness for Gold

Your Vision for Authentic Living

There's a reason you picked up this book: something wasn't working for you; something was holding you back. You didn't read this book to stay in the same headspace, being berated by your monsters and haunted by your skeletons. You came here for change, for a different perspective. You came to know yourself more deeply, to find your inner compass and make sense of the challenges in your life.

When you first stepped foot into this dark house, it may have felt foreign to you – you didn't know your way around, you didn't recognise anything. Gradually, you are becoming more and more comfortable in this place, and in yourself. But with the torch of self-awareness shining bright, you can now see there's still a little more work to do: replacing the tired furniture, the mouldy bathroom and the daggy wallpaper. It's time to repaint those walls and decorate, making this place your own.

Transforming your life is not as simple as cutting out some pictures of a magazine and throwing together a vision board, or coming up with a goal and just expecting that you'll head towards it. If it were that straightforward, we'd all be living the life we want. So far, you've learnt to embrace your darkness – the parts of you and your life that hold you back; you've had to wade through the layers of gunk, spring-cleaning your mind and heart to find connection with yourself, understanding how you've been shaped by past experiences. You've had to let go of some of the baggage that was weighing you down and create space in your life for new possibilities.

Darkness is golden. The parts of you that you once thought were messy, broken or unlovable actually hold hidden gifts. This step of your journey can provide one of the biggest gifts of all. You have the ability to consciously create your life moving forward in a way that is *informed by the journey you have been on.* Rather than relying on some stock-standard interpretation of what a 'successful' life is, or defining it through fear or worry, here you get to decide what is important to you based on *your experiences* and *your needs.* You have done some serious work to figure these out. Now you get to decide what life looks like when *you matter.*

This moment is the culmination of all the lessons you've learnt so far. We are going to take everything you've discovered on this journey and use it all to shape an authentic vision for your life. It's time to make this house your home.

You've witnessed the darkness; now comes the gold.

Solid ground: why now is the time for vision

Look up 'how to create a vision' on Google and you'll get a plethora of sites giving you a step-by-step guide to creating the life you want. I know it;

I've done it. Are they useful? Absolutely. It's a good start to get you thinking. Does it work? Yes and no. It can help you to get what you 'want' but not necessarily what you 'need'. I'm not against vision boards – to be honest, at one stage of my life my entire bedroom wall was covered in goal-lined butcher's paper – but I do prefer a deeper method to creating a vision.

I have intentionally placed this chapter towards the end of the book. Many people starting a transformational journey would expect it to come at the beginning. They might be looking to start with questions like: how do you see your life moving forward? What are your values? What is important to you? What brings you joy? These questions are fine. The issue is without deeper work, you're still answering them from your *existing paradigm*. The monsters, skeletons and spirits that have subconsciously influenced your choices and behaviours would still be there, behind the scenes, pulling the strings without you noticing.

If I start a therapy session with a client creating a vision for their life, I can guarantee it will change by the end of their therapeutic journey subconsciously: we can't put the carriage before the horse. We need to zero in on what's actually going on before we can figure out what the 'right' move looks like.

This is not to say that we can't have an idea of what we want for our future, though. No doubt you picked up this book with *some* idea of what you wanted (e.g. to work on your anxiety, to help you through a break-up, to manage a fear), but coming up with a vision before healing isn't always a great idea. Creating a vision prematurely can cause you to feel even worse about yourself when you fail to make it happen. The disappointment throws you into a world of pain, as you tear down the magazine cut-outs of happy couples, dream homes and Caribbean beaches, convinced it will never happen.

You need to figure out what's holding you back before you jump into action (hello Inner Saboteur). You need to pay attention to your feelings rather than engage in toxic positivity.

Attempting to create a vision without recognising the baggage you're carrying will inevitably lead to disappointment – you don't have the mental or emotional space for it.

You see, most vision exercises get you to figure out what you want at a time when you are most desperate for change (and probably on a mission to get as far away from your feelings as possible). Of course you want comfort and validation when you're down in the dumps. Of course you want the polar opposite of whatever you're going through. Of course you want 'all the things' to be super-productive at work, smashing your career, scoring accolades, fixing your finances, creating a five-year plan. But the reality is, going through a deep and considered transformational journey through your darkness will leave you in a completely different place – one that's more sustainable, and more attuned to your needs. When you've met the Inner Child you learn what your true needs are. And, let's just say, your Inner Child isn't asking for a five-storey house and a tropical island holiday. It's asking for hugs and attention from you.

Letting needs inspire wants

Working with clients has given me a real insight into how people's ideas of what they need, change over the course of therapy. As they transform, they become so much more chill about change – they realise that they don't need to go a million miles an hour and be the overachieving person they thought they wanted to be. They tend towards simplicity and away from ego-orientated accomplishment. They want connected relationships. Their life priorities change. Mirroring post-traumatic growth research (Chapter 1), they want to get off the treadmill of life and actually *live.* This usually surfaces in a desire for deeper relationships, a shift in life goals and values towards altruism and connection. They better realise the importance of self-care, self-compassion and a nurturing connection with themselves, understanding that it is truly the most important relationship they'll ever have.

What I've also noticed is that clients typically come in to work on themselves, but as they progress, they naturally become curious about how they can share what they've learnt with others in a meaningful and sustainable way (rather than from a place of desiring external validation – throwback from Chapter 6). They understand how to validate themselves in their lives and are naturally propelled to give purposefully, while being mindful of their energy. Parents bring practices of mindfulness into their family life, changing the dynamic at home. I see people inspired to start purpose-driven ventures, leave their jobs and start working for (or creating) companies that are doing good things, or start volunteering for causes that matter to them. The once burnt-out CEOs find new ways to connect and inspire the huge numbers of people they work with. Creativity flourishes, even in people who had never picked up a paintbrush or written a song, as clients channel their story through art. Helping yourself can allow you to help others.

What does vision look like without the inner work? One example that comes to mind involves a specific type of client that comes through my doors every so often. This client is typically a high-achiever and involved in some form of philanthropy: think lobby groups fighting child trafficking, climate change startups, or big not-for-profits. They come in with inspiring stories of changing the world and tales of how they've brought their vision to life. They are doing amazing things for humanity and yet they are burnt out, have no time for anything else, and are often depressed. They are completely consumed by their mission in an unsustainable way. Almost always, the journey with these clients reveals that they had been looking for solutions to *their own* internal challenges, by solving the problems of the world. They dreamt big and their dreams arrived. But sure enough, for all their success, they felt more disconnected to themselves than ever. They had put everyone else's needs before their own. It's a narrative arc that resonates with me, as it mirrors my own journey. They have to dig deep so that they can build a vision that addresses their own needs, while helping others. But you? You've now done that work. You're one step ahead.

Let's get disorientated

Creating an authentic vision requires the recognition of your values and priorities as your own creations – that is, different from those that have been forced down your throat through life. To create a successful vision, you need to break down the concepts and models that have been given to you through your family, peers, culture and society. You have to give yourself room to dream. You have to instil what I call a *hypnagogic state.*

***

A hypnagogic state is the slippery, trippy space between wake and sleep, where the rigid structure of our everyday thinking turns molten and thoughts get a little warped and weird. Here, in the land between wakefulness and dreaming, there is no rhyme or reason; imagination runs wild; alien cats play the violin to your boss on stilts.

When we enter sleep, the brain takes apart the structures and concepts we use to make sense of the world and we experience the wonderful and weird possibilities of dreams. The transformational process is similar: you are entering disorientating realms where what was once habitual is being broken down, noticing the rules and constraints you put on yourself. You are unpicking the seams of straitjackets you didn't even know you were wearing, removing the blinkers that shroud your view of the world.

It's important for us to notice that we value what other people value. We value what our families, friends and culture approve of and what media and advertising tells us is cool. Most of us live in an individualistic culture where 'I' is king and 'we' takes a backseat. A place where success often means dollars and accolades, climbing the ladder, likes and followers, influence and power. We rush to have everything 'all sorted out' as adults, as if our plans for the future could offer us security from uncertainty. Once we sift through all these external pressures, we can be free to explore what it means to be authentic to ourselves.

Even though I guide many people through this process, I too have had to learn to remove my blinkers. Until recently I believed that success and happiness were 'just around the corner', as long as I tried harder, stayed motivated and achieved the shit out of everything. I just needed to get there. 'There' was an imagined future place, where I had worked hard enough to become financially stable, had completed my detailed five-year plan and had my shit together.

That elusive 'there' I was trying to get to all my life no longer makes sense to me. I've learnt to embrace that I will never have my shit completely together, and I've let go of thinking that everything is around the corner if only I work hard enough.

I've had to consider what change really means to me: do I really want to be 'better' or do I just want to be more 'authentic'? 'Being better' means living in line with other people's expectations. Being authentic means living for yourself. Our culture is obsessed with 'progress' and 'optimisation', the idea that we should always be moving forward, plan in hand, whether that be in our jobs, careers, relationships or even as humans. In typical personal development, there is a prevailing sense that we should always strive to become 'better' versions of ourselves – more compassionate, calmer, transcendent, balanced and peaceful. But what if life wasn't about being better?

***

Like you, I'm ready for something different. The blinkers are off, and together, we're entering the hypnagogic state. It's time to welcome alien cats, stilted bosses and other-worldly delights.

How to build a vision

Instigating a hypnagogic state in your waking life requires you to step outside your ingrained habits and rebuild the models you've typically relied on to make sense of the world, into something new. When you cast your mind to the weird and wonderful fantasies that emerge as we fall asleep, they are often things we could never imagine – unspeakably creative. If we want to create a world that makes more sense to us, we need to put away our old brushes and pens and wield new instruments. We need to say no to outdated models and expired stories and beliefs and have the courage to create a life that is guided by our authentic values.

Our vision needs creativity, a playful mindset, experimentation and the elimination of our ideas about 'right' and 'wrong'. When we are exceedingly rigid, we fall into the trap of replacing one rigid model for another, closing ourselves to possibilities. In my case, I swapped out working hardcore in my business for going gung-ho in writing this book – it was very much the same model I was using, but a different 'filter'. Rewriting your story, or the stories that have been repeated to you, requires you to take a risk, stepping outside of your comfort zone. Keep this in mind as you create your vision. It's not set in stone. Your vision should shift and change, as you too transform as a person.

Creating a vision is not like making a Christmas wishlist. It's about meaningful change from the inside out, a focus on your psychological needs and helping others sustainably. Bringing anything new into your life requires focus, dedication, energy and maintenance, and we often underestimate how much time and emotional energy it can take to bring a vision to life.

Change can also just be about nurturing, protecting and maintaining your state of being, as opposed to adding more commitments and plans. It can be a shift in *perspective,* learning to see things from a different, more helpful vantage point. Highlighting this shift was a participant from one of my retreats, Vivienne, who got in touch weeks later to tell me that she hadn't had a 'shift' like the other participants – who had left jobs, started new hobbies and made new friends. She said that everything had stayed the same for her in her external life, but her perspective had changed. She now saw things differently. For Vivienne, the job that was once monotonous and draining became less of a bother; it no longer grated on her soul. Relationships felt more enjoyable and she was more patient and easygoing. It was like she was seeing life through a completely different lens, without the smudges of judgement, fears and insecurities that once blurred her vision. She realised how much she had to be grateful for.

When you focus on what you really need, don't be surprised if the answers that you come up with reflect a pared-back lifestyle. Often, personal transformation uncovers a desire for the simplicity that allows you the space to enjoy life more, reflecting a function of not needing to be validated by external forms of success, and more balance in your emotions. If you're a driven person, or someone with a strong sense of purpose, it's important to note that this isn't about taking the fire out of your belly, it's about making sure that fire can stay alight over time. From simplicity grows conscious, sustainable action.

***

There are many things to consider when creating a vision. How do you want to use your emotional energy? What role do you want to play in people's lives? How ambitious do you want to be (or not)? And of course, what is most important and meaningful to you? This process requires you to look at what still may be inhibiting your life, how you want to approach them and what it means for you to allow yourself to dream. Below, let's dissect some areas that you'll want to think about when putting your vision together.

Exercise 1: Reflection

This exercise is designed to take you through the different steps and questions that form the foundation for your vision, reflecting on the journey you have been on throughout this book. It is an invitation to ask yourself the important questions on *how you want to live,* an invitation to welcome meaningful and positive change in your life. Here, we will be bringing it all together.

Write down the answers to these questions in your journal.

Chapter 1

Meeting Your Monsters and Skeletons

- Are there still some beliefs (monsters) that you would like to work on?
- Are there some past experiences (skeletons) that you would like to continue to work on?
- Are there any behaviours that you would like to become more mindful of?

Mindfulness
- What is your favourite way to practise mindfulness?
- What practices and meditations do you want to continue as you move forward?
- How can you envision these pratices as a ritual in your daily life?

Chapter 2
Meeting Your Spirits
- What emotions are you learning how to be mindful of?
- What relationship do you want to have with your emotions, moving forward?
- What emotions do you want to feel more of?
- What body-centric practices will you use to help you get in touch with

your emotions and their sensations (e.g. body scan meditation, dance, yoga)?
• Are there any other purge letters that you need to write?
• How are you honouring grief in your life, moving forward?

Chapter 3
Inner Conflict and the Inner Beings
• Is there any inner conflict that you feel needs resolving?
• How can you maintain a relationship with your Inner Beings?
• How can you practise being more in the Wise Self?
• How can you regularly connect with your Inner Child?
• How can you practise self-compassion in your life?

Chapter 4
Needs, Self-care and Vulnerability
• What are your most important needs?
• How can you meet them through self-care?
• Who will you be practising vulnerability with?

Chapter 5

The Giver
- What boundaries will you be setting?
- Are there other tough conversations that you need to have?
- How can you give more sustainably?

Chapter 6
Rites of Passage and Letting Go
- How can you continue to create meaningful rites of passage to mark transitions in your life?
- Is there anyone else you'd like to forgive?

Chapter 7
Creating an Authentic Vision
- What rules or expectations have you been living by that you want to let go of?
- What values have you taken on from your parents, partner, friends, workplace, society?

What is important and what do you want to prioritise?

Your values are your principles, or standards of behaviour: the things you judge to be important in your life. Along this journey, you may have discovered some new values that are now important to you; there may have been moments and experiences that taught you something or connected you more deeply to yourself and others. Perhaps on this journey you've discovered the importance of getting to know yourself, facing challenges, letting go and building a relationship with yourself, indicating values such as: self-awareness, self-acceptance, emotional intelligence, connection, vulnerability, self-care, self-worth and trust.

Priorities are areas in our lives that we can focus on. Examples of priorities are: family, relationships, career, physical health, mental health, travel, making money, creativity, personal growth.

> Exercise 2: Values and Priorities

This exercise will help you identify the values and priorities that you have gained from this process.

Answer these questions in your journal:

1. What are your values? What have been the meaningful experiences on this journey?

2. What do you want to prioritise in your life? If you could only choose three things in your life to prioritise, what would they be?

Below are a list of values and a list of priorities that you might like to choose from:

Examples of Values:
Accountability
Accuracy
Achievement
Adventurousness
Altruism
Ambition
Assertiveness
Balance
Being the best
Belonging
Boldness
Calmness

Carefulness
Challenge
Cheerfulness
Clear-mindedness
Commitment
Community
Compassion
Competitiveness
Consistency
Contentment
Continuous improvement
Contribution
Control
Cooperation
Correctness
Courtesy
Creativity
Curiosity
Decisiveness
Dependability
Determination
Devoutness
Diligence
Discipline
Discretion
Diversity
Dynamism
Economy

Effectiveness
Efficiency
Elegance
Empathy
Enjoyment
Enthusiasm
Equality
Excellence
Excitement
Expertise
Exploration
Expressiveness
Fairness
Faith
Family-orientedness
Fidelity
Fitness
Fluency
Focus
Freedom
Fun
Generosity
Goodness
Grace
Growth
Happiness
Hard work
Health

Helping society
Holiness
Honesty
Honour
Humility
Independence
Ingenuity
Inner harmony
Inquisitiveness
Insightfulness
Intelligence
Intellectual status
Intuition
Joy
Justice
Leadership
Legacy
Love
Loyalty
Making a difference
Mastery
Merit
Obedience
Openness
Order
Originality
Patriotism
Perfection

Positivity
Practicality
Preparedness
Professionalism
Prudence
Quality-orientation
Reliability
Resourcefulness
Restraint
Results-oriented
Rigour
Security
Self-actualisation
Self-control
Selflessness
Self-reliance
Sensitivity
Serenity
Service
Simplicity
Soundness
Speed
Spontaneity
Stability
Strategic
Strength
Structure
Success

Support
Teamwork
Thankfulness
Thoroughness
Thoughtfulness
Timeliness
Tolerance
Traditionalism
Trustworthiness
Truth-seeking
Understanding
Uniqueness
Unity
Usefulness
Vision
Vitality

Examples of Priorities:
Creativity
Education or learning
Family
Friends
Health and fitness
Income
Influence and power
Making use of talents
Personal growth
Positive impact on society
Prestige and status

Professional growth
Security
Spirituality/faith
Spouse/partner
Stimulating/rewarding work
Time for leisure/relaxation
Travel
Wealth/savings
Where you live

Exercise 3: Creating a Vision

This exercise can help you to distil what your life will look like if you are working towards your vision.

Write down the answer to these questions:

1. What does daily life look like if you are meeting your needs and living in line with your values and priorities? E.g. Would your workplace be different? Would you have the same routine? Would you see anyone more often? These are just a few ideas to get you started.

2. What would you be doing if you embodied all the feelings you want to cultivate?

3. How does your vision involve play? When we're dreaming big, it's easy to forget that we need to leave space for fun in our lives – what does that look like for you? E.g. Painting sessions, joining a football team, hiking, making music.

4. Who would you be surrounded by if you were living in line with your values? You can be specific about the people here or describe the *types* of people you would be surrounded by. What qualities would these people have?

The power of visualisation

Now that you have all the elements of your vision, it's time to help bring them to life by ingraining them in your neural pathways.

Prospection refers broadly to 'the mental representation and evaluation of possible futures', which may include: planning, prediction, hypothetical scenarios, daydreaming and visualisation. Research in this area is pointing to how our visions 'propel' or 'pull' us into the future, as opposed to the past constantly paving our path – we are captains of our future, not prisoners of our past.

Visualisation is effectively tricking the brain into believing that what you are imagining is real, thus creating the neural pathways to support the reality. The brain doesn't know the difference between imagination and reality – they both evoke the same level of emotion. As such, this is a powerful tool to help you get excited about the future and work through any fears that you might have.

Imagine how you can utilise the power of visualisation in your life – to imagine a life where anxiety or depression doesn't control you, to see yourself in healthy relationships, to visualise how you might be able to make a difference in the world.

Now here's something that you may not expect. It's actually essential to visualise the *route* that leads to the outcomes you want in life, not just the outcome. What do you look like *on your* way to achieving these goals? What are signs that you are getting closer? What are you doing? Who are you with? In a series of experiments, students who visualised routes fared better than students who visualised outcomes. This type of visualisation creates a stronger foundation to work from in striving towards your goals.

To help guide your visualisation, I have created a sonic embodiment for you, designed to help you evoke the powerful feelings necessary to create those new neural pathways in your brain.

Audio Experience 8: The Golden Future (11 minutes)

Listen to this audio exercise to help you visualise your future dreams. I recommend listening to this at least once a week to keep you on track with your vision, but you can practise it as much as you like.

During the experience, do your best to allow yourself to feel excited and fulfilled when imaging your vision.

Lie down, put on your headphones and listen to this experience in a quiet place where you won't be disturbed.

> All of the audio experiences can be accessed by the QR code or website at the front of the book. 🎧

Taking action and having accountability

Creating the life you want is all about the small, consistent actions. One small adjustment might be to ask yourself this simple question each morning: 'What is *one thing* I can do today to honour the path that I am on?' By focusing on one thing and having a sense of accomplishment rather than an endless list that you never complete, you set realistic expectations for yourself and are less likely to set yourself up for disappointment. This small habit can help you tune in to what it is you really need that day.

In a study of high-achieving people, Dr Randall Bell discovered that the simple act of making your bed in the morning can have a huge impact on positive mindset, as you begin your day with a micro-accomplishment; it's an accomplishment nonetheless. On the other hand, sometimes, your inner voice tells you that you need a day of rest or play. By listening to this need, you can call your day a 'success' even without any 'accomplishments', and even if your sheets remain bunched in a heap at the end of your bed at 4pm.

Sharing your journey with someone who can help keep you accountable on a weekly basis, whether that be a friend or therapist, can also help you stay on track. When I run courses, in the first class, everyone is paired up with an accountability buddy. The nature of what they're checking in on changes, but it really is as simple as setting a regular reminder in your calendar and sending a quick text message to your accountability buddy. Give it a try – you might like to offer a friend your services for theirs in return. This is especially valuable for personal or creative projects where it's easy to cancel on yourself or procrastinate. If my friend texts me at 5pm every Wednesday reminding me that I committed to go jogging, I'm more likely to go for that jog.

You are not alone

In previous years, my ideas and visions filled walls and decimated packets of Post-Its. I wanted it all: creativity, entrepreneurial success, helping others. I would dive into project after project, each scaling new heights.

One day, I walked into my apartment and collapsed in a heap. I had just co-run a music and mindfulness festival for five thousand people, I'd run a workshop for Spotify in their head office and I was just about to launch my first online course. I looked up at the butcher's paper on the wall and couldn't believe it – of the twenty goals on there, seventeen of them had come true. And I was miserable.

The problem was that my visions didn't account for my emotional energy. Even though I had ticked so much off my list, I felt overwhelmed and exhausted rather than satisfied and accomplished. Upon reflection, I wasn't motivated by the right values. Deep down inside, I wanted my parents to be proud of me, but what I really needed was to be proud of myself.

Burning out more than a few times taught me I had to visualise a life for myself that accounted for my emotional wellbeing. I had to learn to prioritise checking in with myself while pursuing my goals. I had to put my needs first, make sure my Inner Child was alright, listen to my emotions, and learn how to lean on others who could also pull me up when they noticed I was sliding into old habits.

None of that may strike you as particularly inspiring stuff to put in a vision – but I can't stress how much of a difference it's made to my life. It's been a long, hard road learning how to listen to myself and put myself first. It's so easy to see the shiny object and get excited by a vision but I've also learnt that when times are tough, I just need to remember my simple *daily* vision. It's a vision of the simple things: connection with good people, moving my body, eating right, meditation and not trying to 'figure it all out'. I fill my cup in the morning before I give to others.

While I still have big dreams, I tend towards more simplicity in my life these days. I still have goals. Like most of you, I'm still figuring out what I want. I believe it's okay for a vision to have gaps. We don't always need a coherent picture. I'm hoping that these gaps will allow the space for magic, serendipity, play and other unplanned joys. Perhaps it's simpler that I thought – to be content is to want less.

Go easy on yourself

Whatever your vision is, you shouldn't have to sacrifice yourself to make it a reality. It doesn't mean that you don't try. You can't sit back and hope that it falls in your lap. But there is something to be said about learning how to let things be. As I get older, I notice that making a vision come to fruition is often more about being patient than pushing. Remember some of the lessons from your work with emotions and the Inner Beings; we have to learn how to observe our emotions instead of trying to get rid of them, we have to be patient with our Inner

Beings and hear their needs. You've had to learn how to listen to the body, instead of reacting to everything the mind tells you. In that same regard, we need to be patient and learn to trust that our vision will be a reality – but we can't forget to enjoy the here and now.

Remember, 'getting somewhere' doesn't always mean 'smashing it out': replying to more emails, having more meetings, being the productivity police and holding things in a vice-like grip. Panicking about something doesn't make it happen faster, and the juice it takes to run at that speed will flatten any battery. When we hold on to things too tightly, we can strangle them, whether it's new love or our plans for the future.

Slow down and enact change in ways that speak to the movements within you, respecting the tide and flow of your energy sources, your needs in the moment, cutting cords to the 'shoulds'. If you look back on your life, the more you tried to change yourself aggressively and obsessively, the more things stayed the same. And the more you tried to 'rid' yourself of uncomfortable feelings, the more they persisted.

We all want change, at some point. Sure, change can be good. Change can be powerful. But even in those moments when change feels like the answer to everything you're going through, you need to remember – you are enough. Just as you are.

***

You are standing in this house and you are starting to see everything that it could be, all of its potential. You are appreciating every room like never before. Sure, not all parts of the house are perfect, and you've got a good idea of how you want them to be, but you trust that it will get there. You don't *need* the wallpaper to change right away in order to be comfortable here, but you're excited by the prospect of that eventual change.

At its essence, this journey has been about the ability for you to gain perspective on your life and *rediscover who you have been all this time.* To acknowledge all of the parts of you, and to accept them. You are awesome. You are magic. And you are now seeing the true potential for your life. Your visions for the future will no longer be birthed from a dark place of expectations and fear, but from the golden light that shines from the core of who you are, and what you need.

CHAPTER 9

A Thousand Deaths

The Cycles of Change and their Great Gift

Welcome to the final room in the house, the grandest of all. In this room you will meet the ultimate darkness: death. Collect yourself and take a deep breath as you step through this one last doorway. You have entered the ballroom, an ornate space adorned with golden chandeliers and large framed pictures of people who have come in and out of your life. You see the faces of old pets, relatives and friends from your childhood you no longer keep in touch with. The walls are lined with shelves holding small porcelain pots filled with ashes, each engraved with a name of something you have let go of on your journey – the belief that you can't change your life, the part of you that still thinks about your ex wistfully. There's a whole section dedicated to your haircuts. Was that really you? Jesus...

As you stand in this room you recognise that your life has constantly evolved, that you have changed many times over. Here, in the grandest room in your house, you are about to discover the secrets death holds, and how death can be your most important teacher.

Finding meaning by facing death

I'd like to introduce you to a good friend of mine named Fleur. An inspiring woman with a beautiful soul, a high-flying executive, self-declared 'Queen of Busy, superwoman and doing it all'. Ten years ago, she was diagnosed with a rare autoimmune disease called sarcoidosis.

What is fascinating about Fleur's journey is how it mirrors – to the absolute extreme – your journey to face the darkness. Her story begins with the torch of self-awareness nowhere in sight, and in a familiar stage of the grieving process: denial. Fleur ignored the warning signs of her sickness, even to the point where she was coughing blood, telling herself: 'I've just got to get to Christmas and then I'll have a rest.' In these moments, Fleur put everyone else's needs first; listening to her own was not on the agenda.

This continued for the first four years of her illness; she just wasn't accepting it. 'I didn't want to let go of my life. I was a career girl, financially stable, holidays, nice car, and I didn't want to give that up.' She had a – completely understandable – reluctance to let go. Where does one even begin when it comes to letting go of all the things that seemingly define them? Fleur held on to her world with a tight grip.

But reality hit when her diagnosis reached Stage 4. This was the point of no return. In this moment, Fleur realised that she was not going to get her health back. That the world, the lifestyle, the identity she had been clinging to could no longer continue. And so came a profound acceptance of her illness.

As she began to recognise the need to let go, emotions such as grief, guilt and shame bubbled up to the surface: 'I felt like I had done this to myself.' But it wasn't just her external life she had to let go of – Fleur recognised that there were beliefs she held that were holding her back.

The toughest belief to shake was the expectation of what a mum should be: 'I couldn't be the mum I wanted to be. I had to let go of my career and finances and the life I was living ... I was still making the kids lunch at 5.30am even though I could barely stand ... I thought, to be a good mum I had to make lunch. I was working three jobs post-chemo, just to put my kids through private school.'

But the shedding wasn't over. Facing the finiteness of her life, Fleur recognised who her real friends were. Those who were all take and no give had to go. But so too did the part of her that was allowing those relationships to exist. There was no longer space for excess baggage.

Slowly, she became present to her life: 'I dropped my kids off at school and instead of whizzing off as I usually did, I discovered I knew the names of the kids my children were hanging out with.' Her definition of success changed: 'I realised that I had a choice. I could just continue this path of waiting and have it as a blur or I could figure out the life I really wanted. And that's when I gave myself the permission to make the most of my life, no matter how little or long that I had.' Fleur took five months off work to tune in to her needs and figure out what she 'really, really, really' wanted to do.

What is so inspiring about Fleur's approach to her situation is that her prognosis has not changed. In fact, it has worsened. And yet, through the darkest of the dark, Fleur looked within herself and decided that her *perspective* was going to change. She would be more conscious of her choices and decided she 'wasn't going to be the patient' – sure, her disease defined her in some ways, but it wasn't going to take over her identity.

Through the darkness, and by facing death, came an acceptance in which Fleur decided she was going to surrender to the things that she couldn't change or control. 'My disease is my teacher' says Fleur. 'Meaning is what you choose as your perspective. It's how you show up. Your attitude is what keeps you alive.'

We all have a choice in how to see the circumstances of our lives and how to live in the face of them.

The science of facing death

From an evolutionary perspective, the thought of dying is in direct conflict with our biological need to survive. According to psychologists Sheldon Solomon, Jeff Greenberg and Tom Pyszczynski, we repress our fears (or *terror*) of death because of this conflict.

Our repression of the fear of death is a survival instinct: imagine if you lived every moment fearing death? And yet that repressed fear still has a subconscious impact on how we live our lives. In line with Terror Management Theory research, 'Death anxiety drives people to adopt worldviews that protect their self-esteem, worthiness, and sustainability and allow them to believe they play an important role in a meaningful world.'

Our avoidance of pain – insecurity, anxieties, shame, anger, frustration, loss – is also deeply seated in this fear of death. For example, someone leaving you, at the heart of it, reflects a fear that you're unworthy or irrelevant. Feeling the pain of someone leaving you triggers the subconscious fear of dying. When someone belittles us, judges or shames us, for our survival instinct, this is death. Being socially excluded feels like death.

If we are here to learn how to live life to the fullest, then we must explore death. Yes, death is scary and uncertain and there's fear of pain and suffering. But what if we could acknowledge: 'I've only got so much time to enjoy my life. I'm going to make the most of it.'

Life is not endless, yet many of us live as though it is. If you were to truly understand that your time on earth is limited and be reminded of it often enough, do you think you would procrastinate on your dreams as much? Might you think twice about constantly staying back late at work? Do you think that you would value connection with your loved ones more?

Research by professor of psychological sciences, Laura King from the University of Missouri, Columbia, supports this viewpoint. Laura studied life and death from an economics standpoint, her research showing that thinking about death highlights the *scarcity of life,* leading to an increased appreciation for it. Things that are scarce are valued more: the last few hours with someone we love before they leave on a long trip, the near-the-bottom-of-the-tub bit of our favourite ice-cream, the last few squares of a toilet roll when there's no other in sight.

Gratitude for life is also found in people who have encountered a 'Near-Death Experience' where, typically due to coronary arrest, the patient dies but is revived in a relatively short time period. In a study on Near-Death Experiences in a laboratory at The University of Barcelona, Spanish researchers Itxaso Barberia, Ramon Oliva, Pierre Bourdin and Mel Slater found that reports from patients who are revived reflect experiences of euphoria, positive life renewal and happiness. They also report more caring of others and increased concern with universal issues rather than material ones.

Facing your death, or the death of someone you love, is quite possibly the greatest darkness you will have to face at some point in your life. Yet within the dark recesses of death there's a very special gift: the possibility of the most immense gratitude for life you might ever feel and the clearest understanding of your meaning, direction and purpose.

***

Three years ago, I lost my father. He passed away as I began to pen the first chapter of this book and since then his death has played a principal role in my personal transformation. Losing him has been my life-changing moment.

Although I knew my father was gravely ill for a year before he passed away, nothing could prepare me for the way that grief turned up and upended my life – and how his death would also change me for the better.

His death brought to light the ways in which I wasn't living. Back then, it was hard to face the truths of how I was working myself to death and seeking the approval of others through my work. It brought up the root of that pain, the desire to be seen that was unmet, and the resulting ways I tried to be seen in the world that left me burnt out and depressed.

There was a point when I was working maniacally as my dad's health deteriorated, and I was flying back to Vietnam every six weeks to spend time with him: I remember the moment so clearly, looking out on the tarmac before the plane was about to take off towards Ho Chi Minh City. In five days, I'd seen over forty one-on-one clients, run two courses, hosted a workshop, and been interviewed on morning television. Every night, I was managing the business from bed until 2am. I was empty. I remember saying to myself, 'I can't live like this anymore.' I heard the echoes of the words of my therapist, who had tried to warn me about my lifestyle: 'It's a slow suicide, Mary.' It was in that moment that I decided I had to take hold of the steering wheel and careen my life back on course – to change the destination towards authentic living.

Since that moment, I've repeatedly asked myself questions like: *What makes me happy? Where do I want to live? Do I even want to be a psychologist anymore? What is meaningful and important to me?*

For a long time, there weren't any answers, but a glaring need to take care of myself and find my way out of a very dark place. This journey took me through all the same challenges that you have faced as you've worked your way through this book. I had to write a letter to my ex. I had to cry. I had to awkwardly call my friends and tell them I was feeling alone. I had to sit in feelings that I was a terrible boss when I delegated the piles of work I could no longer keep up with. I had to build a life where I mattered. I had to show up for myself. I had to let facing death teach me how to live.

A meditation on death

During the period of my father's illness I became involved in a multidisciplinary project called *We're All Going to Die,* a festival created by film director Stefan Hunt which brought together expressions of death through music, dance and art, inspiring people to 'fear less and live more'. My role was to create a death meditation – an experience that could help participants reflect on death in a way that stimulated a new appreciation of life moving forward. Creating 'Death Meditation' was a work of love and a cathartic experience – it transformed my confusion and grief into an experience that could help people navigate death in a meaningful way.

A death meditation has origins in Tibetan Buddhism and typically involves a closed-eye visualisation of the deterioration of one's body as one dies – the stages of decomposition that occur. According to Buddhist monk Venerable Pende Hawter, meditation on death is regarded as very important in Buddhism for two reasons. Firstly, 'It is only by recognising how precious and how short life is that we are most likely to make it meaningful and to live it fully' and secondly, 'By understanding the death process and familiarizing ourself with it, we can remove fear at the time of death and ensure a good rebirth.' I wanted my experience to leave people with an understanding of how they could change their lives moving forward.

Creating an experience that replicates death is not simple (no-one has lived to tell the story). I had, however, experienced my own death at a sacred ayahuasca ceremony. Ayahuasca, an Amazonian plant medicine, is a psychedelic medicine that can show you different realities. It has been used for centuries for healing and insight. These experiences are difficult to communicate, but in my 'death experience', it was as if I had truly left my body and travelled into the spirit world. I could no longer feel my body and existed as a disembodied consciousness. I was asked to face death. I had to 'accept' that I was never going to see my friends again. That I would never hug my partner, that I wouldn't be turning up to work the following Monday. It was a lot to take in. Was I proud of the life that I had lived? Was there anything that I regretted not doing, saying or letting go? These are some of the thoughts that accompanied the experience, and I was beyond grateful that I was alive when the medicine wore off and I was back in my body. The insights gained set the tone for the death meditation that I subsequently created.

In my research I also discovered that some of my thoughts in my ayahuasca experience mirrored those of the dying. Bronnie Ware, a palliative care nurse, explores five regrets expressed most commonly by those at the end of their lives in her book, *The Top 5 Regrets of the Dying:*

I wish I'd had the courage to live a life true to myself, not the life others expected of me;
I wish I hadn't worked so hard;
I wish I'd had the courage to express my feelings;
I wish I had stayed in touch with my friends;
I wish that I had let myself be happier.

It appears that facing death ignites a reflection on one's life, with the realisation that sometimes we can take it for granted. I wanted 'Death Meditation' to hold space for a reflection on these possible regrets but before our time on our deathbed.

When we think about death, one question that might come to mind is: what matters in the face of death? Does it matter that we have cellulite on our butts or that we didn't get many likes on our last Instagram post? Does it really matter what other people think of us? Or how much money we have in the bank?

I penned much of 'Death Meditation' by my father's bedside during his final days. As he lay in bed, hooked to oxygen and IV drips, I contemplated this rite of passage that we all take at the end of our lives. Death ripples far beyond the life that is extinguished. It lights a candle for anyone who wants to guide themselves to their own truth of what it means to live.

***

At the premiere of 'Death Meditation', participants entered a darkened room, then lay on the ground with noise-cancelling headphones that played the sound journey. As people filtered out into our reflection space afterwards, I saw people hugging their friends tightly, and others calling their parents and loved ones. 'Death Meditation' was a wake-up call. People realised they were living their lives on autopilot, and gained insight into how they wanted to live moving forward. It shattered the illusion of endless days and never-ending relationships, but it also gave people hope that they could live their lives with meaning – and inspired them to change.

I still listen to 'Death Meditation' on occasion. It reminds me to stop taking my life, and those around me, for granted. It reminds me to let go of the fears that hold me back from living authentically, to open my heart. It reminds me that I matter and that I deserve to live my life with purpose. To be real, I bawl my eyes out every single time I hear it.

The night that 'Death Meditation' premiered, my dad was in hospital in an induced coma, on a mechanical respirator. He never knew about the 'Death Meditation', how my journey with his death inspired it or how it helped so many people. He died a week after the festival, before I could get back to Vietnam to see him.

***

You do not need to wait until you are ill, or walking the path with someone who is dying, to awaken the potential of wisdom that death can hold in your lives. If you choose to see it, death really is a gift in disguise, a celebration of life, an agent of change.

Audio Experience 9: Death Meditation (21 minutes)

Death Meditation is a powerful sonic embodiment designed to help you orientate your life towards more meaning and purpose, to appreciate your life and your loved ones.

This sacred and profound rite of passage was originally presented as a ceremony.

To mark the ritual, create a ceremonial space for yourself. Dim the lights and light some candles. Note that this ceremony can also be experienced with some of your closest friends. You will require some headphones, pen and paper, and a quiet place where you won't be disturbed. It is best experienced lying down so you can fully relax. (You might also need some tissues.)

Note that you may experience a range of emotions, like sadness and fear, as you will be exploring your vulnerabilities. It is recommended that you have at least half an hour of reflection time afterwards, to allow the full effects of the experience and time for reflection.

This experience may not be suitable for people who are recently bereaved. Give yourself some space to heal, and come back to this at some point in the future.

All of the audio experiences can be accessed by the QR code or website at the front of the book. 🎧

Reflecting on 'Death Meditation'

Is there someone you feel pulled to connect with, just to let them know that you care about them? If there is, put down the book and *do it.* If you get a nudge like this during 'Death Meditation', respond to it.

Perhaps you have realised that you need to let yourself off the hook for something you've been feeling guilty over or that there is something that is holding you back from living the life you want. Perhaps you have realised that you need to appreciate yourself and know that you are enough. Perhaps you've had a wake-up call that will lead you to the start of a new cycle, the beginning of a new story that will help you love more and learn to connect more deeply to yourself and others. When the seas become rough, I hope this book is something that you can come back to again and again, to give you strength and hope in all the shades of darkness and light of your life.

Death and a perspective on your path

The shadow of death has been cast across your entire journey. You may have come to this book because there was a part of you that had experienced a 'death' in the form of loss. This may have been the loss of a dream – like where you thought your life might be right now. It may have been the ending of a relationship, a job or a way of life because of unforeseen circumstances such as the global pandemic. You may have felt compelled to take this journey because you *needed* to experience the death of a part of you that no longer served you – an attitude that life was meaningless, a belief that you were not enough, a way of overworking or anxiety that drained you.

Think back to Chapter 3, where we explored the unmet grief of your painful past experiences. Do you remember the ones that you felt? Your grief reflected the acknowledgment of the pain that comes with change and in turn paved the way for your transformation.

Take a moment to remind yourself...
What have you grieved on this journey?
What have you let go of?
What have you let in?
What has replaced the things you've let go?

You have shed layers of yourself, old patterns that shackled you, to make space for the new you. You have found the expiry date on limiting beliefs that were thriving in the darkness. Beliefs like: *I'm not good enough.* Into the fire they went, to be replaced by golden, empowering beliefs like: *I am enough.* Every step towards your vision is you stepping into your authentic self. In every change you have actioned, you are accepting the death of the old and the cultivation of the new.

***

My favourite quote is from Buddhist monk Pema Chödrön:

To be alive, fully human, and completely awake is to be continually thrown out of the nest. To live fully is to be always in no-man's-land, to experience each moment as completely new and fresh. To live is to be willing to die over and over again.

The message in this quote implores us to embrace the discomfort of the deaths within us as we move through life, shedding what once gave us comfort so that we can grow and appreciate the life we have.

This is what you have done. A thousand times over. A thousand deaths.

The cycles of change

Accepting that the cycles of change are inevitable helps you be prepared for your path moving forward. The reality is, life will continue to be messy at times. There's no *up* without a *down*, no autumn without spring, and you too will experience the continual cycles of change. Like renovating a house, tending to the garden of our lives can feel endless – like there is always something else to fix.

Challenges will come, many outside of your control. And in those moments, your mind will continue to do the thing that it's built to do: judge your actions or thoughts, attempt to keep you safe and tell you things about yourself that you don't always want to hear. There will be times when you feel in control, grounded and self-aware, and other moments when all hell breaks loose and you feel as though you're back at the beginning of your journey. You might find that a pattern of yours flares up, perhaps jealousy or insecurity in a relationship or imposter syndrome at work. You may get consumed with anxiety and feel lost and disconnected again. Exasperating as it might feel, I can't stress how normal this is. I still wake sometimes with morning anxiety and wonder what I am doing with my life, then remind myself to listen to some music, meditate and say hello to my monsters, skeletons and spirits.

Often, I feel differently by the time lunch rolls around.

The difference is, you now have the tools to navigate these challenges. You can always open up the backpack of wisdom you've been filling on this journey and ask yourself: 'What do I need to let go of so that I can move forward? What needs to die so that I can transform? What beliefs are driving my feelings? What am I avoiding feeling?' At the heart of your frustration and fear you will find something that you are holding on to, something you're afraid of letting go of or afraid of feeling. Step back and observe it by embracing this new challenge.

You are learning to live your life from a place of truth, honesty and integrity. You are learning how to be willing to face these deaths, over and over – not from a place of sorrow, but from a place of acceptance. Take solace in the knowledge that the challenging times will pass. Although it may feel like you have more to 'fix' within yourself, the path of life is not about being wrapped up in yourself, consumed with endless tinkering or tuning. Like the tides, we also need ebb and flow – to move between discipline and action, into softness, rest and play.

You are not alone

To some, this may not feel like the triumphant way that books and films are supposed to end, but to me, it is so much more. Throughout this book you have faced the 'thousand deaths of you' – your skeletons, pain, grief, traumas and anxieties. You've met your corners, your edges, all the places that you've shied away from for most of your life. It's a big deal. As a rite of passage, your transformations have been no walk in the park. You've learnt to face yourself and your past, to test your resolve and trust. And you accomplished this without a cheer squad but with the growing chorus of your own internal validation. I have been so honoured to share part of this journey with you. You've learnt how to truly live and make the most out of your life, walking through your darkness knowing that you are not alone in these dark moments.

You have travelled deep into your memories and psyche and developed an understanding of the complexity of your life's experiences as best you can. This is the development of *meaning:* making sense of who you are, what the world is like and how you fit into this grand picture. You wield the power to write the script of your life.

***

In the Japanese art of *kintsugi*, pieces of an accidentally broken pot are put back together with reverence and respect, carefully joined with a beautiful gold lacquer that accentuates the lines of breakage. It is a reflection of the Zen Buddhist philosophy of *wabi sabi*, which honours impermanence, simplicity and the perfection in imperfection. There is something beautiful about the attentiveness and honour that is given to the process of repairing something that most people would discard or try to hide.

Like the pieced-together pot, we are not broken pieces to be discarded. We don't need to be ashamed of our experiences and we don't need to hide our anxieties or sadness. These 'broken pieces' of us have value regardless of how negative they might feel or appear. In the process of meeting our darkness and our 'thousand deaths', we can find our own process of *kintsugi,* piecing ourselves together with care and respect, highlighting the ways these cracks and moments of healing have changed us for the better. What were once aspects of ourselves that we wanted to keep in the dark – our anxieties, fears, traumas and grief – can be celebrated. You are still whole, useful, even beautiful, with your 'imperfections'. These golden 'scars' are like lines of a map illustrating the roads of where you have travelled deep within yourself.

***

Take a deep breath and see this in your mind's eye. There is an enormous dining room table that runs through the middle of this ballroom. It has been set with embroidered cloth, candles, flowers and overflowing cornucopias of food – a meal fit for a royal. You notice a card at the head of the table with your name written on it and you take a seat. A vinyl record begins to play. It's your favourite song. You crack a smile, intrigued but unsure. And then, all at once, the doors burst open. The volume goes up. In pour all of the characters you have met along this journey.

Your skeletons roll in, screaming the lyrics as they pop the corks on giant bottles of prosecco. Your monsters jump up onto the table and begin dancing. One of them starts to twerk. (A bit much, but you're okay with it.) Your spirits float around the chandeliers, present but not bothering you. In fact, you do not feel afraid at all. You're happy to see everyone. As you sit at the head of this table, you come to the realisation that this is a celebration of you. All of you.

Your Inner Beings take their seats at the table – the Giver, the Inner Child, the Saboteur, the Inner Critic – and charge their glasses, proposing a toast. A toast to you. For who you are, exactly as you are. For the journey you've taken. For the attention you have given to yourself. From behind you, you are wrapped in the warmest, most loving hug you have ever felt. It is your Wise Self. And into your ear, it says ... 'You can wear your "gold" proudly. This is who you are. Look around you. These are your stories, your triumphs, your tenacity. This is your vision. This is how you become a positive force in your world, encouraging others to look and listen within themselves as well. You are enough. You are never alone. Through the cycles we travel together, seeking wisdom in the shadows. Whenever you're ready to be with all of us, to welcome us to the party, to accept us, we are here for you. Home is always beckoning – it lies within you.'

CONCLUSION

Homeward Bound

Growing up, there was a flight of stairs in our family home that led from the kitchen to the bedrooms on the next floor. It was a wooden spiral staircase, one that wouldn't be out of place in a warlock's lair. At night, I was terrified of walking up the creaky, windy stairs, convinced that a spirit was pursuing me in the dark. My hairs would rise at the nape of my neck and, feeling the panic of something chasing me, I'd always bolt up the stairs, outrunning the 'ghost'.

Throughout my life, I've often dealt with my fears in a similar way: by running away from them. It never occurred to me that I could have faced my fear of those dark stairs, nor the other challenges in my life. It was only through the lessons of wise teachers – psychologists, monks and shamans – that I realised that nothing would change unless I undertook their teachings: to face and feel what I perceived as my darkness in order to heal and transform. I never knew how powerful it could be to explore everything that I felt compelled to ignore until I started seeing the shifts in myself and, as a therapist, within others.

Most of us have never known that we have to *face* the darkness in order to *conquer* the darkness.

We've travelled through our lives believing the monsters in our heads, being ashamed of the skeletons from our past, and afraid of the spirits of our emotions. We've asked ourselves, 'Who am I?', 'Who can I become?' and 'How can I change my life?', unsure of where to find the answers. We've carried beliefs that we are broken, unfixable and unlovable because of past experiences. We've ignored the child within us who is afraid of the dark. We've run away from ourselves.

But something has changed: *you*.

Your transformation has been like a series of interconnected dark rooms. By opening this book you built up the courage to take your first step into the dark. Do you realise how brave that was? Slowly, your eyes began to adjust and you switched on the torch of self-awareness. Exploring this room with your torch – under the dusty couch, in cupboards you've never opened – you shed light on the things you have been avoiding – your monsters, spirits and skeletons.

It wasn't easy to uncover them, but now you can see them: the pesky thoughts, the unruly emotions, the threads of the past. It's easier to recognise them when they waltz into your life and run riot like rock-and-roll stars in a hotel room. Knowing that they're going to make a bit of a mess is better than running after them and berating them – besides, they only get more unruly when you try to control them. You've learnt that eventually your creatures will tire out if you just let them do their thing. You see them, you feel them, you understand where they have come from. Every time you do this, you are practising self-acceptance.

In the next room, you met your Inner Beings: your Inner Saboteur, Inner Critic and Inner Child. You sat on the couch and chatted with each one of them. You heard their stories; you held their hands. You understood why they were in your life and thanked them for their protection. Each time you understood where they were coming from, you saw the Wise Self grow in you: the holder of wisdom, truth and compassion. You now know that in times of inner conflict you can always confer with the Inner Beings – they are not foes but friends who are always trying to help you. When you give them love, you are guided by your Wise Self – your inner compass.

In understanding the journey of your Inner Beings, you were handed another gift: the knowledge of your unmet needs – social connection being just one. Here, as you learnt to apply self-care and express your vulnerability to those close to you, the light of the room brightened with the glow of connection and self-awareness.

Travelling to the next room, you found yourself overrun with clutter and the messiness of relationships. You met the Giver, the part of you that puts others first and desires validation. In conversation with the Giver you have discovered why this part of you was in the dark – it feels unworthy and wants to be acknowledged. In this room you learnt how to accept the Giver in you. You realised your worth, learnt how to practise healthy boundaries and became clearer in expressing your true needs. Each time you practised this you cleared some of your clutter and grew your self-worth.

You could barely get through the next doorway, and when you did you found yourself tripping over with every step. What were all these obstacles? As you felt around in the darkness you realised that you were in a room with all of your baggage: your collection of resentment and insecurities from past relationships. This room was piled high with old memorabilia and photos – there was hardly any space to move around! It was time for a big clean-up. You lit candles and spring-cleaned, throwing out what you didn't need. This was tough. But gently, you let go of past relationships, dropped baggage, and made space for possibilities and a vision for your future.

And finally, you entered the darkest, most beautiful room of all, where you met death. You faced the death that had walked with you throughout this journey as you said goodbye to old patterns and behaviours. You considered the world without you in it. When you did this, you felt the appreciation for your life, the skin that you're in, the people you love and the world at your feet.

***

What was once a collection of neglected, messy rooms has been transformed into a shining house full of light. Each room has represented parts of you that you've typically disowned and rejected. But now that you have shone the light of self-awareness through each, they are places where you can feel more comfortable. You now have your bearings – you know where things are kept. You're not stumbling around in the dark anymore. Turns out, everything you needed was always there, waiting for you to see it.

Now, there's just one final thing that I would like you to do.

You deserve a house-warming. I encourage you to get a few of your closest friends and show them around, share your experiences with them. Show them how you've grown and changed. Tell them some of the stories from each room and the lessons and gold that you've discovered. This is your honouring ceremony. Think of it like a graduation or a tribal gathering where you are initiated into the next phase of your life. This is your final rite of passage for this book. Like the tribe around the dancing Apache girls, these are the people who will remind you of your resilience and strength in times of struggle.

You deserve to be acknowledged.

You could have turned around. You could have continued to sleepwalk through life. You could have taken one glimpse at this neglected house and said, 'No way'. But you didn't. You recognised that something had to change. You willingly stepped inside and faced your darkness.

Close your eyes and allow yourself to fully embrace the feeling of being proud, of valuing yourself, of being worthy. Bask in the warmth of appreciation for yourself. Hold close the things that you are most grateful for in this life.

***

This house of light is your creation. When you step back, it is an incandescent vision, a reflection of your life and what makes you, you. It still has its shadows and cobwebs. There are undoubtedly trap doors and secret attics you've yet to explore. Lightbulbs may blow, blackouts may happen. But when everything seems to fade to black, you can trust that the golden guiding light you seek lies right there, in the darkness.

The house you once considered haunted is now transformed.

Welcome home.

WORKS CITED

Introduction

1. 'The scariest thought in the world...' Saunders, George, http://www.oprah.com/omagazine/george-saunders-favorite-books/all
2. Krause, A.E., Scott, W.G., Lucano, R. & Hoang, M., 'Focused listening: An examination of Listen Up experiences', paper presented at the 2019 International Symposium on Performance Science, Melbourne, Australia, July 2019
3. Krause, A.E., Skeffington, P., Hoang, M. & Lucano, R., 'Exploring sonic embodiment experiences', manuscript in preparation, Department of Psychology, James Cook University, 2020

Chapter 1

1. Van der Kolk, B., *The body keeps the score: Brain, mind, and body in the healing of trauma,* Viking, New York, 2014

2. Mcleod, S., 'Systematic desensitization – a treatment for phobias', https://www.simplypsychology.org/Systematic-Desensitisation.html, 2020
3. Turrell, J., *Backside of the moon,* Benesse Art Site Naoshima, Japan, 1999, https://benesse-artsite.jp/en/art/arthouse.html
4. Goldsmith, Oliver, 'Our greatest glory...', https://www.quotes.net/quote/1214, accessed 2020
5. Solomon, R. & Higgins, K., *Reading Nietzsche,* Oxford University Press, New York, 1990
6. West, Kanye, Bangalter, T., de Homem-Christo, G., Birdsong, E., 'Stronger', *Graduation,* Roc-A-Fella Records & Def Jam Recordings, 2007
7. Clarkson, Kelly, Elofsson, J., Tamposi, A., Gamson, D., Kurstin, G., 'Stronger (What Doesn't Kill You), *Stronger,* RCA, 2012
8. Linley, P. & Joseph, S., 'Positive change following trauma and adversity: A review', *Journal of Traumatic Stress,* 2004, 17(1), pp.11–21

9. Collins, R., Taylor, S. & Skokan, L., 'A better world or a shattered vision? Changes in life perspectives following victimization', *Social Cognition,* 1990, 8(3), pp.263–85
10. Schwartzberg, S., 'Struggling for meaning: How HIV-positive gay men make sense of AIDS', *Professional Psychology: Research and Practice,* 1993, 24(4), pp.483–90
11. Rendon, J., 'Post-traumatic stress's surprisingly positive flip side', *New York Times online,* 22 March 2012, https://www.nytimes.com/2012/03/25/magazine/post-traumatic-stress-surprisingly-positive-flip-side.html
12. Tedeschi, R. & Calhoun, L., 'The posttraumatic growth inventory: Measuring the positive legacy of trauma', *Journal of Traumatic Stress,* 1996, 9(3), pp.455–71
13. Tedeschi, R.G. & Calhoun, L.G., 'Posttraumatic growth: Conceptual foundations and empirical evidence', *Psychological Inquiry,* 2004, 15(1), pp.1–18

Chapter 2

1. Achor, S., *The happiness advantage,* Ebury, London, 2011
2. Noor, I., 'Confirmation bias', https://www.simplypsychology.org/confirmation-bias.html, 10 June 2020
3. Medium, 2020, Cognitive triangle image, https://medium.com/real-life-resilience/the-cognitive-triangle-bdc4eb08a4f5
4. Fenn, K. & Byrne, M., 'The key principles of cognitive behavioural therapy', *InnovAiT: Education and inspiration for general practice,* 2013, 6(9), pp.579–85
5. Bradt, S., 'Wandering mind not a happy mind', https://news.harvard.edu/gazette/story/2010/11/wandering-mind-not-a-happy-mind, 11 November 2010
6. Killingsworth, M. & Gilbert, D., 'A wandering mind is an unhappy mind', *Science,* 11 November 2010, 330(6006), p.932
7. Bargh, J., 'Our unconscious mind', *Scientific American,* 2013, 310(1), pp.30–37

Chapter 3

1. Boyce, C., Daly, M., Hounkpatin, H. & Wood, A., 'Money may buy happiness, but often so little that it doesn't matter', *Psychological Science*, 2017, 28(4), pp.544–46
2. Wilson, T. & Gilbert, D., 'Affective forecasting', *Current Directions in Psychological Science*, 2005, 14(3), pp.131–34
3. Eisenberger, N., 'Meta-analytic evidence for the role of the anterior cingulate cortex in social pain', *Social Cognitive and Affective Neuroscience*, 2014, 10(1), pp.1–2
4. Gross, J. & John, O., 'Individual differences in two emotion regulation processes: Implications for affect, relationships, and wellbeing', *Journal of Personality and Social Psychology*, 2003, 85(2), pp.348–62
5. Gross, J., 'Antecedent-and response-focused emotion regulation: Divergent consequences for experience, expression, and physiology',

Journal of Personality and Social Psychology, 1998, 74(1), pp.224–37
6. Gross, J. & Levenson, R.W., 'Hiding feelings: The acute effects of inhibiting negative and positive emotion', *Journal of Abnormal Psychology,* 1997, 107(1), pp.95–103
7. Impett, E.A., Kogan, A., English, T., John, O., Oveis, C., Gordon, A., Keltner, D., 'Suppression sours sacrifice: Emotional and relationship costs of suppressing emotions in romantic relationships', *Personality and Social Psychology Bulletin,* 2012, 38, pp.707–20
8. Gross, J. & Levenson, R., 'Emotional suppression: Physiology, self-report, and expressive behavior', *Journal of Personality and Social Psychology,* 1993, 64(6), pp.970–86
9. Ekman, P., 'Are there basic emotions?', *Psychological Review,* 1992, 99(3), pp.550–53
10. Ekman, P., 'In search of universals in human emotion,

with Dr. Paul Ekman' [video], 2008, https://www.exploratorium.edu/video/search-universals-human-emotion-dr-paul-ekman
11. Quoidbach, J., Gruber, J., Mikolajczak, M., Kogan, A., Kotsou, I. & Norton, M., 'Emodiversity and the emotional ecosystem', *Journal of Experimental Psychology: General,* 2014, 143(6), pp.2057–66
12. Sutton, A., 'Living the good life: A meta-analysis of authenticity, wellbeing and engagement', *Personality and Individual Differences,* 2020, 153, p.109645
13. Roberts, Geoffrey, '"I Feel" – Emotional Word Wheel', Imgur, 2020, https://imgur.com/gallery/q6hcgsH
14. Morgado, F., Betanho Campana, A. & Fernandes Tavares, M., 'Development and validation of the self-acceptance scale for persons with early blindness: The SAS-EB', *PLoS ONE,* 2014, 9(9), p.e106848

15. Ackerman, C.E., 'What is self-acceptance? 25 exercises + definition and quotes', 2020, https://positivepsychology.com/self-acceptance/
16. Body-outline image, Pinterest, 2020, 'Blank Body: Body Outline, Body Template, Human Body Diagram', https://www.pinterest.com.au/pin/559572322433518274/
17. Kübler-Ross, E. & Kessler, D., *On grief and grieving,* Simon & Schuster, London, 2014
18. Chödrön, Pema, *When things fall apart,* Shambhala Publications, Boulder, 1996

Chapter 4

1. Morvan, C. & O'Connor, A., *An Analysis of Leon Festinger's A Theory of Cognitive Dissonance,* Series: Macat Library: Great Works for Critical Thinking, Routledge, New York, 2017
2. Iyengar, S. & Lepper, M. 'When choice is demotivating: Can one desire too much of a good thing?',

Journal of Personality and Social Psychology, 2000, 79(6), pp.995–1006
3. Holmes, T., Holmes, L. & Eckstein, S., *Parts Work,* Winged Heart Press, Kalamazoo, 2007
4. Schwartz, R. & Sweezy, M., *Internal Family Systems Therapy,* 2nd edn, Guilford Publications, New York, 2019
5. Overs, Jessica, Graphic designer, 'Boardroom of Inner Beings' [diagram]
6. Neff, Kristin, *Self-compassion Exercises by Dr. Kristin Neff,* 2020, https://self-compassion.org/category/exercises/

Chapter 5

1. 'Maslow's Motivation Model' [illustration], Ilic, Biljana & Stojanović, Dragica, 'Management of employee motivation for successful business in the banking sector', *Progress in Economic Sciences,* 2018, 5(5):111–25
2. McGuire, K., 'Maslow's hierarchy of needs', GRIN Publishing, 2012

3. Mcleod, S., 'Maslow's hierarchy of needs', https://www.simplypsychology.org/maslow.html
4. Denning, S., 'What Maslow missed', https://www.forbes.com/sites/stevedenning/2012/03/29/what-maslowmissed/#6d4ae33a661b
5. Rutledge, Pamela B., social model diagram, 'Social networks: Where Maslow's Hierarchy of Needs model misses', *Gestalt Therapy,* 2020, https://www.google.com.au/amp/s/gestalttherapy.wordpress.com/2012/10/30/social-networks-where-maslows-hierarchy-of-needs-model-misses/amp/
6. Brown, Brené, *Daring greatly: How the courage to be vulnerable transforms the way we live, love, parent, and lead,* Avery, New York, 2017 edn

Chapter 6

1. Bourne, E., *The anxiety & phobia workbook,* New Harbinger Publications, Oakland, 2010

2. Jeffers, S., *Feel the fear and do it anyway,* Vermilion Life Essentials, London, 2019 edn

Chapter 7

1. Ashworth, Dr D., 'How have intimate relationships changed over the years, and where does it leave us now?', 2016, https://damonashworthpsychology.com/2016/05/24/how-has-romance-changed-over-the-years-and-where-does-it-leave-us-now/
2. Cherlin, A., 'Marriage has become a trophy' 2018, https://www.theatlantic.com/family/archive/2018/03/incredible-everlasting-institution-marriage/555320/
3. Rubinstein, A., *The making of men,* Brio Books, Sydney, 2013
4. Grimes, R., *Deeply into the bone,* University of California Press, Berkeley, 2000
5. Scott, H. & Wepener, C., 'Healing as transformation and restoration: A ritual-liturgical exploration', *HTS Teologiese Studies/Theological*

Studies, July 2017, 73(4), http://www.hts.org.za
6. Broadly staff, *Inside an Apache rite of passage into womanhood* [video], VICE Life, 3 February 2018, https://www.vice.com/en/article/qveded/inside-the-sacred-ceremony-that-ushers-apache-girls-into-womanhood
7. Gennep, A., *The rites of passage,* Routledge, London, 1977 edn
8. Cayoun, Bruno, '7 steps to effective communication: Mindfulness-Integrated Cognitive Behaviour Therapy Foundations Course', MiCBT Institute, Hobart, Australia, https://mindfulness.net.au/

Chapter 8

1. Roepke, A. & Seligman, M., 'Depression and prospection', *British Journal of Clinical Psychology,* 2015, 55(1), pp.23–48
2. Kappes, A., Wendt, M., Reinelt, T. & Oettingen, G., 'Mental contrasting changes the meaning of reality', *Journal of Experimental*

Social Psychology, 2013, 49(5), pp.797–810
3. Bell, Randall, *Me We Do Be: The four cornerstones of success,* Owners Manual Press, USA, 2017

Chapter 9

1. Chödrön, Pema, *When things fall apart,* Shambhala Publications, Boulder, 1996
2. Pyszczynski, T., Greenberg, J. & Solomon, S., 'A dual-process model of defense against conscious and unconscious death-related thoughts: An extension of terror management theory', *Psychological Review,* 2016, 106(4), pp.835–45
3. *Psychology Today* (online magazine), 'Terror management theory', 2020, https://www.psychologytoday.com/au/basics/terror-management-theory
4. King, L., Hicks, J. & Abdelkhalik, J., 'Death, life, scarcity, and value: An alternative perspective on the meaning of death',

Psychological Science, 2009, 20(12), pp.1459–62
5. Barberia, I., Oliva, R., Bourdin, P. & Slater, M., 'Virtual mortality and near-death experience after a prolonged exposure in a shared virtual reality may lead to positive life-attitude changes', 5 November 2018, https://journals.plos.org/plosone/article?id=10.1371/journal.pone.0203358
6. Ven. Pende Hawter (ed.), 'Death and dying in the Tibetan buddhist tradition', Buddha Dharma Education Association, http://www.buddhanet.net/deathtib.htm
7. Ware, B., *The Top Five Regrets of the Dying,* Hay House, New York, 2019 edn

Mary Hoang creates transformational experiences grounded in psychology and music to help people heal and evolve. As an entrepreneur, artist, head psychologist and founder of mental health organisation The Indigo Project, Mary is tearing down the walls of traditional psychology and finding inventive ways to help people navigate life.

After her father's death in 2017, Mary turned to art and writing to explore how the darker aspects of life hold the keys to insight and purpose. Exhibiting at Vivid Sydney, the Art Gallery of NSW and festivals throughout Australia, Mary's powerful art installations take the form of contemporary rites of passage.

Sound plays a vital role in Mary's work. She has developed a unique format of audio experiences called 'sonic embodiments', created alongside composer Phondupe (Rich Lucano). These moving experiences informed ground-breaking research with the University of Melbourne on the positive impact of music on mental health.

Mary is excited to be embarking on a new adventure into psychedelic-assisted therapy and is currently working with the Southern Hemisphere's first training program in the field.

She believes that the majority of challenges can be solved with a good plate of pasta.

Darkness is Golden is her first book.